Shut Up and Look Pretty

A dating manifesto for soft power and high standards

Crystal Carmen Caple

Caple Legacy Group

COPYRIGHT

"The woman who never rushes always arrives exactly where she intended."

Author's Note

If you find your story echoed in these pages, know that I kept you anonymous for a reason. Please don't take offense. Everything I share here is said with love and with the desire to see you win , in life and in love.

I may be blunt at times, but it comes from a place of wanting you to live your best life. The truth is, "soft life" and "safe love" have levels. They don't look the same at every age, every stage, or every income bracket. What they do share is this: a softer, more secure, and more indulgent life surrounded by love, peace, and alignment.

The stories, examples, and lessons here are not about judging or exposing anyone. Names and details have been changed to respect privacy. The point is not who these stories are about, but what they reveal about the patterns we all face in relationships.

So think of me as your dating bestie. We're sitting together, maybe over good food, a glass of wine, or a cup of tea, and I'm telling you the truth, plainly, lovingly, and without sugarcoating. Because you deserve to feel safe, honored, and adored, and the sooner you know what that really looks like, the sooner you'll stop settling for anything less.

Dedication

To Ryan, my partner in love, life, and every late-night brainstorm that kept me going. You carried boxes, calmed storms, made me laugh when I wanted to cry, and reminded me who I was when I almost forgot. This book carries your fingerprints as much as mine.

To my friends and family, who cheered me on in more ways than they know

Joey, Sophia, Metsy, Anna, Tisha, Kamira, and Rose thank you for celebrating every milestone and getting almost as excited about this book as I have. Your love, laughter, and encouragement made this journey lighter, brighter, and unforgettable.

To my Vanity Image Clients, the women who sat in my chair and shared their stories, their struggles, and their wisdom. You trusted me with your beauty and left me with pieces of your truth that shaped these pages.

To my dating clients, past and present, you are living proof of what happens when women choose themselves and trust the process.

It has been incredible to witness the engagements, the new relation-ships, and even the weddings that grew out of our work together. Knowing that my coaching helped you leave toxic love behind and step into the kind of partnerships you truly deserve has been one of the greatest honors of my life.

To every woman who has ever asked me for advice since I was sixteen you are the reason this book exists. You trusted me to help you notice patterns, leave cheaters, stop cheating yourself, and learn to love the real way.

To the women I've met for moments or hours, the brilliant, high-functioning, successful women who seem to have everything handled yet still long for peace and partnership this is for you too. I once read a book that helped me shift my behavior a little, but nothing like what I share here. I thought: what if women like us could finally find the love we seek? The kind of love where you can let your hair down, breathe, and be held. Where a man gently closes the laptop at night so you can rest and then takes something off your plate so you don't feel guilty about it. The kind of love where you finally get a little peace and a lot of love.

PREFACE

Three Rings. Three Lessons

I've been married three times.

The first? It doesn't even count. It was a marriage built on all the wrong reasons, the decision you make when you're young, unhealed, and trying to fill a void. I thought the title "wife" would fix something in me, it would provide security for my daughter, but all it did was shine a light on how empty that foundation really was.

The second? This marriage was for what I believed was for all the right reasons. It felt purposeful. I believed in it. And for a while, it really worked. But as I grew into it, as I started learning who I truly was beneath all the noise and roles I had taken on, the marriage began to unravel. Sometimes it's not that the love wasn't real, it's that you outgrow what you once needed. And that's a truth nobody prepares you for.

The third? That was a smack in the face. Not because it was a mistake, but because it forced me to live out everything I had been teaching other women for years. By the time I entered that relationship, I had finally developed a mindset and dating strategy that shifted my focus inward. For once, it wasn't about what I was to someone else, it was about who I was to myself.

Each marriage taught me something different:

The first taught me what happens when you don't know yourself.

The second taught me what happens when you do, but you stop honoring that truth.

And the third taught me that healed women date differently and they marry differently too.

This book is not just advice pulled out of thin air. It's a collection of lessons I lived, repeated, cried through, and finally broke free from. I've helped women leave cheaters, stop cheating themselves out of love, and finally figure out why things weren't working so they could experience real love, not survival love.

And that's what this book is about: guiding you on stepping out of patterns that no longer serve you, so you can date with strategy, love with intention, and finally see yourself as you were always meant to.

Because once you heal, everything changes.

PROLOGUE

I didn't write this book to tell you how to be prettier. You already are. I wrote this book because too many women are sitting at the bar of life, sipping on watered-down attention, waiting for someone to choose them, when really, the choice is theirs.

This is not another book about "rules." It's a playbook for soft power. It's about walking into any room, whether it's a cocktail lounge, a first date, or your own living room after a fight with your husband , and knowing that you have control over the energy, the outcome, and the vibe.

I've been the girl who was single and trying to figure out why it wouldn't work out. I've been the wife holding together a marriage when everyone else said it was over. I've been the woman side-eyed for being "too much", too ambitious, too loud, too sexy, too soft. And I've learned that when you stop explaining yourself and start embodying your worth, the whole dating game changes.

So think of this book like me sliding onto the barstool next to you, whispering the secrets no one told you, clinking my glass with yours, and saying: "Baby, you're about to date differently."

And yes, I met my husband at a bar... But that's a story for later. This book is about YOU and the power you're about to unlock.

CONTENTS

THE MOST EXPENSIVE DECISION YOU'LL EVER MAKE

The High Cost of Thinking You Know Everything

Women will spend weeks hunting for the right couch, months test-driving cars, and years planning degrees for themselves or tutors for their kids. They'll research brands, read reviews, compare options, and consult experts.

But when it comes to the most expensive decision of all, who they will share their life with, suddenly, discernment flies out the window. Suddenly, it's: "Well, he's a little nicer than the last one. He's not as bad as my ex. "He's kind of cute". He took me on a couple of dates."

Honestly, that's not discernment. That's desperation disguised as "good enough." And it's one of the most costly mistakes a woman can make.

Because the truth is this: the man you choose can magnify your life, or he can drain it. He can be your peace or become our prison. And if you think you know everything, if you think you don't need any guidance, research, or support, you're playing Russian roulette with your future.

We Research Everything Except Love

Think about it. We'll spend 3 weeks researching a car before signing a loan. We'll tour 10 apartments before moving in. We'll agonize over fabric samples for a couch. We'll send our kids to ballet lessons, pay for private basketball coaches, hire a math tutor, enroll in tennis classes.

In every other area of life, if we want something to work out, if we want to get better faster, we hire a coach, we take a class, we invest.

But when it comes to love? Suddenly, women give it the bombastic side eye. Suddenly, "I got this, I don't need help."

Crystal's Confession

"Let me tell you something that still cracks me up. I've had women take me to lunch, acting like they just wanted to catch up. And then halfway through, they start pulling out their messy love lives like it's show-and-tell, hoping I'll evaluate it for free. One time, a friend asked me to lunch, then casually added another woman to the table. And it didn't take long to realize why. She wanted her friend to get a mini-coaching session off my plate. It wasn't lunch. It was an emotional ambush."

Now, did she do it intentionally to devalue me? I don't think so. But that's not the point. Because at the end of the day, if I need what you have, then I will pay you for the service. Nobody questions swiping a card for a hairstylist, or tipping a bartender, or paying a trainer to get their body together. But when it comes to love, the most expensive, most consequential area of our lives, suddenly paying someone for their expertise feels... wrong.

That's exactly why so many women keep losing in love. Because they won't invest time nor money in it the way they invest in everything else.

The Hidden Cost of Pride

Here's the truth: if you can't honor expertise, you can't attract excellence.

The same women who will funnel free advice out of me are the same women who complain they keep attracting low-effort men. Of course they do. Because you can't vibrate on "I want everything for free" and expect to attract a man who values generosity, investment, and abundance.

The energy is the same. If you can't respect value, you won't recognize it in a man.

Better Than the Last Is Not a Strategy

Too many women measure new men against old ones instead of measuring them against their values.

- He's not as mean as my ex.

- He's not as broke.

- He's not as emotionally unavailable.

That's scraping the bottom of the barrel. That's using a failed relationship as your benchmark instead of using your standards as your guide.

You don't pick a college major because it's "better than the last job you hated." You don't buy a house because it's "not as bad as the last one you rented." So why are you choosing men that way?

The Real Price of the Wrong Man

Let's talk about cost.

- Financial: The wrong man can tank your credit, drain your savings, and keep you stuck paying for everything while he contributes nothing.

- Emotional: He chips away at your confidence, makes you doubt yourself, and rewires your brain to think "this is all I deserve."

- Physical: Stress kills. Neglect shows up in your body. Anxiety breaks down your immune system.

- Opportunity: Every year you waste with the wrong man is a year stolen from the right one.

I've said it before: being lonely in a relationship is worse than being lonely while single. Because when you're single, the solitude is yours. But when you're partnered and unseen, that's a prison.

Crystal's Confession

"I remember the hours I put into researching business contracts, product ingredients, packaging, every tiny decision in my companies. I triple-checked everything. I compared competitors. I studied the details. And yet when it came to love, I didn't always put that same energy into discernment when I was younger. Sometimes a little attention, a few sweet words, or a couple of dinners was enough to convince me someone might be right. And those shortcuts cost me more than any failed business deal ever did."

Don't Be Afraid to Ask for Help

The women who win in love are not the ones who "know everything." They're the ones who are humble enough to ask for help.

If you're holding this book, I already know you're not one of those women who side-eye dating coaching. You're open-minded. You're hungry for more. And let me tell you: that open mind is already half the battle.

Because you can't demand what you can't sustain. You can't say you want a high-value man but refuse to do the work on yourself. You can't say you want alignment but reject every piece of feedback or guidance.

And you definitely can't build the future you want by recycling the same man in a different body over and over again.

Location Matters Too

Sometimes, it's not even about you. It's about where you are.

"If I hadn't moved from Bethlehem, Pennsylvania, the butterfly effect would've never let me meet my husband . That move changed everything for me. It aligned me with opportunities business and personal that I never would have had if I'd stayed stuck. Sometimes the reason you're not meeting the right man isn't because you're unworthy , it's because you're fishing in the wrong pond."

That's why you need guidance. That's why you need research. Because sometimes your block isn't who you are, but where you are

The Truth Bomb

This is the most expensive decision you will ever make. Bigger than your house. Bigger than your career. Bigger than your couch, your car, your vacation, your degree.

The man you choose can cost you everything, or he can give you everything. And if you think you know it all, if you think you don't need support, if you think "better than the last" is enough, you will pay for it.

Crystal Carmen Real Talk

Don't freeload in love. Respect expertise the same way you do in every other area of life.

"Better than the last" is not discernment. It's desperation. Raise your standards.

The wrong man costs more than the wrong house, car, or job ever will. Don't gamble with your future.

Love is an investment. Research your man like you research your money moves.

The right man is never confused about wanting you. If he's leaving you in limbo, he's not it.

Journal Prompts

Have I ever spent more time researching a couch or car than I did evaluating a man? What did that cost me?

Do I measure new men against my values, or against my last relationship?

Where in my life have I tried to get "free" advice instead of investing in real guidance? How did that reflect in my love life?

If I treated love like the biggest investment of my life, what would my non-negotiables be?

What area (location, mindset, habits) might be holding me back from meeting the man I want?

Embracing Your Feminine Essence: The Art of Shutting Up and Looking Pretty

L et's get one thing clear: feminine energy is not about being passive, submissive, or weak. It's about tapping into a power that doesn't need to shout to be heard or force to be felt. It's the kind of energy that enters a room and shifts the entire vibe, without lifting a finger.

And somewhere along the way, too many women were told that femininity meant being small, soft-spoken, or dependent. Or worse, they were told to "toughen up" and "be more like a man" just to survive. That's survival energy, not seduction energy. And baby, I'm here to get you back to thriving.

This chapter is your mirror. A soft, sexy, empowering mirror that reminds you who you are when the makeup's off, the bra's flung across the room, and you're just... you. Fully expressed. Fully magnetic. Fully feminine.

This is where your journey begins.

"Don't keep auditioning for love like it's a role in his life. You are the script."

DEFINING FEMININE ESSENCE

Let's ditch the Pinterest quotes and go deeper. Feminine essence isn't about wearing pink and being "nice." It's about receiving. About flowing, not forcing. About creating and connecting with emotion, intuition, and truth.

You are both soft and powerful. Emotional and logical. Delicate and unshakeable. Your feminine energy doesn't compete, it completely owns the space she's in because she knows she doesn't have to earn her worth. She is the worth.

Think of it like this: masculine energy is the bouncer, protective, structured, alert. Feminine energy is the vibe inside, the velvet, the mood lighting, the slow music, the allure. And you? You're the champagne on ice. You don't chase. You get chosen.

THE INNER QUEST: SELF-REFLECTION

Now let's go internal. Embracing your feminine essence means knowing who you are, not just what you've been through.

Ask yourself:

- What do I value in life and love?

- What makes me feel radiant?

- What parts of me have I muted to make others comfortable?

You can't call in high-value love while running on low-vibration beliefs. Start unlearning. Start releasing. That "strong independent woman who doesn't need anybody" thing? Cute on paper, exhausting in practice. You're allowed to receive. You're allowed to be supported.

NURTURING SELF-COMPASSION & SELF-LOVE

Let me be blunt: You can't glow if you're constantly dimming yourself with self-criticism. Self-love is not a face mask and a mimosa (although those help). It's how you talk to yourself. It's the boundaries you keep. It's the way you stop apologizing for taking up space.

Your femininity needs softness. It blooms in kindness, not perfection. That means trading "Why am I like this?" for "Of course I feel this way." It means choosing rituals over routines, pleasure over pressure.

Treat yourself like the prize and watch how others start treating you.

RECONNECTING WITH YOUR BODY AND EMOTIONS

Your body is not just a thing you drag through the day. It's a sensual, intuitive, powerful compass. When you reconnect with it, magic happens.

Start slow:

- Stretch in the morning and feel your curves.

- Dance in the kitchen to a song that makes you feel dangerous.

- Tune into your emotions without judgment.

Sensuality doesn't start in the bedroom. It starts in the mirror. In the shower. In the quiet way you run lotion across your collarbone and feel it. Stop rushing. Start feeling. That's the gateway to your feminine power.

Crystal's Confessions

I had a friend who constantly attracted these wishy-washy, emotionally unavailable men. The type who wanted all the perks of a relationship, like her help, her body, her loyalty, without ever truly committing. She was the queen of over-delivering. Always helpful. Always filling in the gaps. Always trying to earn love. I told her straight up: "That's masculine energy, doll. You're out here doing all the work and calling it love; you cannot be the driver for both sides of the relationship.

One day she called me, notably upset and frustrated. Yet another man had cheated on her, this one with his ex. And this time, she finally saw the truth: he would always put everything and everyone before her. It hurt to hear this happened to her, but I also knew she deserved so much more. I told her she could find someone who loved her in a new and holistic way.

Thankfully, that was her wake-up call.

Once I encouraged her to stop auditioning for the role of "ride or die" and just let herself be a woman: soft, intuitive, magnetic, everything changed. She attracted a man who loves her, provides for her, and shows up for her emotionally. She left income-contingent housing, became a thriving nurse, and is now in a healthy, grown-woman relationship on fact, the last update is that she is currently engaged.

Let that be your reminder: the right man doesn't need you to prove anything. He just needs you to be fully you. Feminine. Glowing. Unbothered. And whole.

UNLEASHING CONFIDENCE & ASSERTIVENESS

Let's get one thing straight: being feminine doesn't mean being a pushover. You can be soft and still say "No." You can be sweet and still walk away when someone doesn't value you.

Confidence in your feminine energy isn't about being the loudest woman in the room. It's being the one with standards.

Say what you mean. Ask for what you need. And don't shrink to fit into anyone else's comfort zone.

EMBRACING VULNERABILITY

Here's the truth: vulnerability is hot. Not messy, not needy, hot. It's magnetic. It's how we connect.

You don't have to be the "cool girl" who never catches feelings. You're not ice. You're honey. Stop hiding your heart behind sarcasm and shutdowns.

You're allowed to say, "I need to be held right now." That's not weak. That's real. And real love can't find you if you're busy pretending you don't need it.

THE FEMININE IN RELATIONSHIPS

In healthy relationships, feminine energy attracts masculine energy. It's not about control, it's about polarity.

Let him lead sometimes, but only if you trust where he's going. Let yourself receive without guilt. Be soft without fear. And if he can't hold space for your softness? He's not the one.

The right partner will protect what you reveal, not exploit it. That's the standard now.

FEMININITY IN YOUR CAREER & GOALS

Your softness is not a liability in the workplace, it's a superpower. Emotional intelligence? Sensual presence? All of those create a magnetic influence.

You don't have to grind yourself to the bone to be successful. You can lead with warmth. You get to create beauty and impact. You get to build a life that feels like silk, not sandpaper.

Ambition and femininity are not enemies. They're dance partners in this thing call life.

Coming back to your feminine essence doesn't mean you never had it. You were born with feminie energy, and it isn't about changing. It's about remembering. Reclaiming. Returning to the part of you that always knew you were magic.

You were never meant to hustle 24/7, to settle for crumbs of something, or to harden yourself to survive. You were meant to glow.

And now, it's your time.

CRYSTAL CARMEN REAL TALK

- Femininity is power, not passivity. Stop playing small to make others comfortable.

- You don't have to chase. You attract when you're aligned in your heart and your actions.

- Self-love isn't a vibe, it's a standard. Act like the prize, it will make you do prize things and you'll be treated like one.

- Your softness is sacred. Your intuition is legit. Your vulnerability is divine.

- If being in your feminine feels foreign, it's not because it's not you. It's because you've been too busy surviving to remember. Remember, survival is not just about trauma, it's about feeling like you are the only thing or person that you have been able to rely on, so it feels safe and familar.

JOURNAL PROMPTS

Where in my life have I been operating in survival mode instead of feminine flow?

What limiting beliefs do I have about femininity that no longer serve me?

Who taught me to associate femininity with weakness, and how can I rewrite that story?

What parts of my sensuality have I been hiding and am I ready to bring them back?

CULTIVATING CONFIDENCE

B ecause confidence isn't a look. It's an energy. And yours is about to be undeniable.

Confidence isn't about being the loudest woman in the room. It's about being the one who doesn't need to explain why she's worthy.

Let me be blunt: confidence is sexy. Not the kind you fake in selfies or slap on like lip gloss, but the kind that comes from knowing who you are, what you bring, and what you're not putting up with anymore.

You don't need everyone to like you. You need to like yourself so damn much that the room either rises to meet your vibe, or gets out of your way.

This chapter is your permission to stop second-guessing yourself and start walking like the prize. Because you are. And you've been sleeping on your own magic for way too long.

Let's wake her up.

THE FOUNDATIONS OF SELF-AWARENESS

Real confidence starts with self-awareness. Not filters. Not titles. Not what you do for other people. It's knowing:

- What lights you up

- What drains your soul

- And what you're no longer available for

This means you take inventory of your own patterns. Are you confident, or are you just surviving? Are you assertive, or just performing strength while dying inside?

Confidence means radical self-honesty. You don't need to be perfect. You just need to know yourself better than anyone else.

CELEBRATING PERSONAL ACHIEVEMENTS

Listen, I don't care if the world clapped for you or not, you've done some sht worth celebrating.

Women are so quick to move the goalposts. You hit one milestone, and boom, you're onto the next, still feeling like you're not enough. That ends now.

Celebrate yourself:

- You left that toxic relationship? Celebrate.

- You held it together through heartbreak, burnout, and breakdowns? Celebrate.

- You got out of bed today and didn't text that man who drained your energy? Babe, that's a win.

Confidence doesn't come from being flawless. It comes from stacking small wins until you trust your own power again.

OVERCOMING SELF-DOUBT & FEAR

Self-doubt is a liar with a loud mic. And fear? She's got a whole playlist.

But here's the truth: confidence isn't the absence of fear. It's just the decision to move, anyway.

I need you to stop asking, "What if I'm not ready?" and start asking, "What if this actually works out better than I imagined?"

You are not the same woman you were a year ago. Stop living like she's still in charge.

THE POWER OF POSITIVE THINKING

I know, I know, positive thinking sounds like some Pinterest board fluff. But let me say it plainly: your thoughts are orders to the universe.

What you say about yourself matters. What you believe about your future matters more.

Start speaking like a woman who knows she's next in line for something divine. Because you are.

And no, affirmations don't work overnight. But try spending one week saying:

- I'm magnetic.

- I trust my energy.

- I don't chase. I align.

... and then tell me the energy around you hasn't shifted.

BUILDING CONFIDENCE THROUGH COMPETENCE

Here's the not-so-sexy secret about confidence: sometimes it just comes from getting better at something.

Learn. Practice. Improve. Reinvest in your glow-up mentally, emotionally, financially. Take a class. Hire the coach. Read the damn book.

Confidence blooms where competence grows. You don't need to be the best. You just need to know you're growing.

CULTIVATING INNER RADIANCE

That thing people can't put their finger on when they meet you? That's radiance. It's the inner glow of a woman who's done her healing and is living in her truth.

It's in how you laugh. How you speak. How you take up space without apology.

Radiance can't be bought. But it can be cultivated. Through rest. Through pleasure. Through boundaries. Through joy.

Light doesn't need permission. Neither do you.

COMMUNICATION AND ASSERTIVENESS

Let me say it louder: You can be kind and still mean every word you say.

Stop watering yourself down. Say what you want. Say what you need. Say what you won't tolerate.

Being assertive isn't aggressive. It's clarity. And clarity is sexy.

FACING SETBACKS WITH RESILIENCE

Confidence isn't built in your best moments, it's built when everything falls apart and you choose to rise, anyway.

You will get rejected. You will fail. People will misunderstand you. And guess what? You'll still win.

Because when you're truly confident, you stop seeing setbacks as signs to stop, and start seeing them as the training ground for something bigger.

EMBRACING YOUR INNER RADIANCE

Radiance isn't reserved for models, influencers, or women with six-figure skincare routines. It's for you.

Right now.

With your past. With your doubts. With your realness.

Confidence is quiet. It's sacred. It doesn't need to announce itself. It just is.

You don't need to become anything more to be radiant. You just need to be more of you.

Let me tell you something personal.

Years ago, I worked in the plus-size modeling and fashion community. And in the beginning? It felt amazing. Empowering. Like I was part of something bigger, changing the game for curvy women and claiming our space in beauty and fashion.

But the more I stayed, the more I saw the truth.

Behind the scenes was a lot of cattiness, shade, and backstabbing. The community was supposed to be about inclusion and support, but what I witnessed was a crab-in-a-barrel mentality. Instead of collaborating, people were competing for a spotlight and stepping on others to get there.

Even worse? I started seeing how people were being financially taken advantage of. It stopped being about empowerment and started feeling low-vibrational. It was toxic, manipulative, and dishonest, and no amount of money or clout was worth my continuing to be associated with that.

So I quiet quit. No announcement. No drama. I simply stopped aligning with what no longer served me and took my creativity, my energy, and my integrity elsewhere.

And guess what? I still do my thing. I still make magic. And I have zero apologies about it.

That, my love, is confidence. It's not just walking into rooms like you own them, it's having the self-respect to walk away from the ones that no longer match your frequency.

CRYSTAL CARMEN REAL TALK

- Confidence isn't a performance, it's a decision.

- You don't have to feel ready to be ready.

- The glow isn't in the glam, it's in the healing, the clarity, and the boundaries.

- Stop downplaying your wins. They're the bricks in your foundation.

- Your radiance is not up for debate. Walk like it's already done.

JOURNAL PROMPTS

What does confidence feel like in my body, my voice, and my energy?

What story have I been telling myself about not being "ready"?

What past win am I long overdue to celebrate?

Where have I been hiding my radiance, and why?

For Plush Sized Women and Moms...

Here's what a lot of dating coaches, podcasters, and "passport bros" conveniently leave out of their conversations:

You don't have to be stunningly gorgeous or a size 6 to find real love and a good man or not have children.

I'm 315 pounds on any given Sunday, and I'm married. So are 90% of my full-figured friends and colleagues.

Your energy is the basis. Period.

I'm not saying don't present yourself in your best light, you should. But don't dress like you aren't hot, because you are. Your thighs will be thick in sweatpants or in a skirt, so you might as well show up like you know it.

Men love a woman with exhilarating confidence. Not cockiness, confidence. It's that energy that makes you smile wider, shine brighter, and walk with a magnetism that takes you up a notch.

And let me say this clearly: do not believe the hype of the angry podcasters and the bitter men who want to fly overseas looking for someone "easier." Let them go. Their departure does not diminish your value.

Because if you're a good woman, already confident, already showing up with the right spirit, then love is out there for you, regardless of your weight or "traditional" looks.

Crystal Confessions

If you're slim, own that ish. If you're thick, let it be. I'm not perfect, and I don't pretend to be.

Men are not obsessed with "perfect." They are drawn to women who look arranged. That's the root of the word cosmetics, from *cosmo*, meaning "to arrange in order."

Being arranged doesn't mean you're flawless. It means you've put thought into your presence. You cared enough to show up like you matter. And that makes all the difference.

If there's something about yourself you just can't get past, something that keeps you sulking or stuck, then fix it. Book the filler. Get the facial. Do whatever will make you remember who the heck you really are. Because once you believe it again, you'll radiate it again.

And the truth is: love doesn't belong to the perfect. It belongs to the confident.

Single Mom Energy: Don't Believe the Hype

I have four children. Yes, four. And let me tell you something, having kids doesn't make you any less worthy of love.

As a trauma survivor, I understand the hesitation about bringing people around your children. And I'll be real with you: anybody can be a problem, including the biological parent. That's why discernment matters.

But please don't buy into the narrative that being a single mom means you have to settle for scraps. That's another lie society loves to push.

Here's the truth: out of a sea of men, not every single one will be okay with you having kids, and that's fine. That's what the law of averages is about. It only takes THE one. One genuine man who shows up consistently, who you can watch over time, who proves through his behavior that he's trustworthy, respectful, and safe for you and your children.

Having kids does not erase your value. It only means the man who chooses you has to be the right fit. Think about it: do you want a man who loves hunting if you're vegan? No, that's not alignment. Same with kids, it's preference and compatibility.

Crystal Confession

If you're dating toward marriage, understand this: once he becomes your husband, he becomes your children's stepfather. That means he has a say in discipline, in structure, in the household. Taking away the phone, grounding, setting boundaries, those are leadership roles.

So don't make that move lightly. Don't invite someone into your home, your life, and your children's lives unless you are ready to allow him to lead in that fashion.

And when you do meet the right one? Don't shrink. Don't question if you're "too much." Remember, you are not less because you are a mother. You are more.

Safe Love Sparks Growth

Anybody who takes a scroll through my social media, many years back as you like, can see photos and evidence and proof that I show up to events wearing whatever I want. Whether it be a crop top, a miniskirt, a ball gown, or an evening gown, the point is, I'm going to show up the way that I want to.

I'm going to be confident, and I've done this. I've been over 300 pounds for at least the last 3-5 years.

Approximately a year ago, I decided on my own, to ask my husband if it was okay if I went to the gym with him. We then set forth on a journey since Jun. Today, I am more toned, I'm more fit, I can breathe better. All the swelling in my legs left. I started eating differently, working out differently, focusing more on ingredients. And guess what? I only lost 15 pounds out of the whole thing because I was 330 when I started, but I feel amazing. I have significantly more muscle and less fat.

I am sharing this with you to point our that I decided to become more fit on my own. Watching his desicpliine insoipred me to to invest in my fitness. He never once told me to go to the gym with him or that I had to lose weight or, said "Hey, you sure you want a second serving of that?" Never.

I did it on my own. So the right relationship and the right environment can actually provide the safety that allows you to start taking the time to take care of yourself but they have have to love you as your are first.

Your size does not define your desirability, your looks to not determine your worth in a relationship, your children do not disqualify you from love, and real love does not demand that you change. The right man provides safety, and in that safety, you make blossom and grow.

Crystal Carmen Real Talk
Your size does not define your desirability.
Being "arranged" is more powerful than being "perfect."
Having children does not disqualify you from love.
The right man respects both you and your family.
Real love never demands you change,it gives you the safety to grow.

Journal Prompts
How do I want to "arrange" myself today in a way that reflects my worth?

Where have I been believing lies about my size, my motherhood, or my value?

What does confidence look like for me in action, not just in words?

If I were to stop settling, what would I require in a partner for myself and my children?

How has safety (or lack of it) in past relationships shaped the way I care for myself today?

Your Accolades and Accomplishments Are Not Bargaining Tools

High-vibrational, Highly Intentional men aren't hiring, so stop pitching your résumé.

Let me get this straight: I'm a published beauty editor, a dating scientist, an award-winning business owner, and a woman who's raised children, built brands, survived hell, but still walks in softness and style. But I had to learn this the hard way.

None of that makes me easier to love.

Your achievements don't disqualify you of course but they also don't *guarantee* connection. They don't automatically attract safety, commitment, or adoration. Especially not from a truly masculine, high-vibrational man.

Men who lead with their worth, don't need to prove it, and women who lead with their accolades are often secretly afraid they won't be chosen just for being them.

Let's be clear: being accomplished is powerful. You worked hard, you sacrificed, you earned those degrees, built that business, paid off the debt, and became the strong, resilient woman you are today. That is something to be deeply proud of.

But when it comes to love? That résumé? It's not your leverage. It's not your value. And it's not your selling point.

A high-vibrational man does not want to date your LinkedIn profile.

He wants to date YOU. Your softness. Your joy. Your authenticity. Your ability to connect, not just your capacity to grind at work or your business.

Sometimes we lead with our accomplishments because we're afraid we're not enough without them. We want someone to choose us because we're impressive, not realizing that real love isn't impressed by pressure. It's awakened by presence. It is your presence, your energy, your tenderness that makes a man feel at home.

A man who's emotionally grounded and spiritually aware? He's not sizing you up like a recruiter.

He wants to know:

- Are you safe to love?

- Can he relax around you?

- Will you nurture peace or spark power struggles?

A man who is rich in mind, emotional intelligence and resources doesn't need another job applicant. He needs a woman who knows her power without needing to flaunt it.

Crystal's Confession

Let me tell you when it really hit me.

I was in the thick of my boss era, pulling in over 6 figures. Business was booming. Clients were on waitlists. I was winning awards, being featured, and doing everything I said I would do.

But I would go home and feel unseen.

Not unloved, unseen.

And it broke me.

Because here I was thinking, "How can I be this successful and still be this lonely?"

I'd walk into rooms where I was the prize... and go home to a relationship that made me feel like a placeholder.

I thought success would fix it. If I just worked hard enough at being a better me or had more income it would change.

But all success did was put a spotlight on how emotionally underfed I was.

That's when I realized.

Accolades and accomplishments don't fix misalignment.

You can be the baddest woman in the room and still feel spiritually starved if your relationship doesn't know how to nourish your soul.

That was the moment. The pivot point for me?

Not the day I hit my first five-figure month.

Not the day I won that award.

The day I whispered to myself, I want more and I am willing to be alone until I find I what I find that level of alignment, even if that means I never do. At least it would not be self-betrayal.

Leaving wasn't about punishment. It was about alignment. It was about freeing myself from proving anything to anyone and creating space for a love that could match my evolution.

Crystal Carmen Real Talk

So no, your accolades are not baggage, but they are not your main bargaining chips.

Let your glow be the magnet, not the grind.

Let your softness speak louder than your résumé.

And let your accomplishments be the crown you wear, not the chain you carry into every first date.

Because the truth is this:

A healed man will love you for who you are, not what you've earned.

He'll see the power in your rest. The beauty in your joy. The magic in your surrender.

And when you're ready for that kind of love... your achievements won't be the prize.

YOU will be.

Journal Prompts

What did success not fix for me emotionally?

Do I feel safe in love to be unpolished, undone, or unsure?

In what ways have I used my achievements to shield myself from rejection?

What would it feel like to attract love without performing?

What kind of relationship would support the real me, not just the successful me?

Am I willing to let go of being impressive so I can be intimate?

What part of me believes love has to be earned?

Emotional Intelligence: Understanding and Expressing Feelings

B ecause your feelings are valid, but your delivery makes all the difference.

Let's keep it cute and honest emotional intelligence is a non-negotiable for a high-value woman. It's the difference between reacting and responding. Between chaos and connection. Between pushing a man away and inspiring him to protect your heart.

So many women claim they want a mature relationship, but they still argue like a teenager who just got her phone taken away. You can't build intimacy by emotionally detonating every time you feel triggered.

In this chapter, we're getting into the real work. How to understand your emotions, express them without popping off, and connect
to the man you want without losing your damn mind.

WHAT IS EMOTIONAL INTELLIGENCE?

Emotional intelligence is your ability to recognize, understand, and
manage your own emotions, and to navigate other people's emotions
with empathy and tact.

There are five key elements:

1. Self-awareness

2. Self-regulation

3. Motivation

4. Empathy

5. Social skills

If that sounds clinical, don't worry. You already have it in you. You
just need to refine it.

Being emotionally intelligent means knowing when to pause before
you speak, how to communicate your needs without blame, and how
to own your feelings without making them someone else's fault.

FEELING WITHOUT FALLING APART

Let me be clear: your emotions are not the enemy.

But your lack of emotional regulation? That's where the sabotage
lives.

You are allowed to feel everything, rage, fear, sadness, joy, desire.
But when you don't learn to hold those feelings without turning them

into weapons, you become unsafe to connect with. For yourself and for others.

You want to be magnetic? Learn how to sit in discomfort without spinning out. Learn how to say, "I'm feeling this way, and I'm giving myself space to feel it," instead of spiraling into accusations and shut-downs.

Crystal's Confession

There was a time when I was reacting purely out of emotion. I didn't know how to regulate, I just needed to say something. To feel heard. To not feel so overwhelmed by what I was experiencing.

But I realized something powerful: my emotional outbursts weren't bringing him closer. They were pushing him away.

What I really wanted was connection... but what I was creating was disconnection. I could feel it. My tone, my words, my energy, it wasn't safe. Not for me, and definitely not for him.

That's when I learned the power of slowing down and communicating with intention. I started using phrases like,

"When you do X, it makes me feel Y,"

or "This may not be what you meant, but this is how I'm receiving it."

It's humbling. It's not always easy. But it's so much more effective.

Staying calm doesn't mean silencing yourself. It means expressing yourself in a way that keeps the door open, for resolution, for intimacy, and for growth.

EXPRESS WITHOUT EXPLODING

It's not about avoiding your feelings. It's about channeling them.

You want to be taken seriously? Speak with calm clarity. No insults. No threats. No emotional tantrums. Just truth, softness, and timing.

Because yes, timing matters.

You don't drop emotional bombs when he's drained, distracted, or in problem-solving mode. That's not emotional intelligence, that's sabotage dressed in "I just want to talk."

If you want to be taken care of, speak like someone worth taking care of.

CONNECT WITHOUT COLLAPSING

A lot of women confuse vulnerability with emotional dumping.

They want to "be real" but end up being raw,   reckless,   and confusing.

Here's the difference:

- Vulnerability says, "Here's how I'm feeling, and I trust you to see me."

- Emotional dumping says, "Here's my emotional mess, now fix it."

The first builds intimacy.

The second builds resentment.

And let's talk about trauma dumping, because yes, it needs to be said.

Sharing your entire life story in the first few calls or dates is not bonding. It's bypassing boundaries. You may feel connected, but it's a false sense of intimacy, and it's one-sided.

He didn't earn that level of access to you yet. And now you've emotionally exposed yourself without knowing if it's safe.

Your story is sacred. Your pain is not a conversation starter. Emotional intelligence means knowing how to pace emotional disclosure, not throwing it at someone like a test.

Let the connection unfold like silk, not a spill.

EMPATHY IN ACTION

True emotional intelligence includes empathy, and not just for him. For yourself.

Ask yourself:

- Am I giving myself grace for how I feel?

- Am I offering compassion, or am I criticizing myself for having emotions?

Empathy also means holding space for how he feels. If you want to be met with tenderness, lead with it.

You'd be surprised how many men would open up more, if they felt safe to do so.

Woman to Woman

Emotional intelligence in a woman is critical.

Too many women sabotage good connections simply because they haven't mastered the art of timing, tone, and emotional control. There is a time and place for everything.

You want him to lead? Then be mindful of when and how you speak to the man you want to care for you. Asking for something while he's drained or distracted won't lead to elegant outcomes.

Express what you feel, yes, but do it calmly. Without attacking. Without accusing. Without coming in hot.

You don't need to raise your voice to raise your value.

CONCLUSION

Emotional intelligence isn't about being perfect, it's about being powerful with your emotions instead of powerless to them.

You don't need to suppress your feelings. But you do need to master them.

Because the most irresistible women are the ones who can be soft and self-aware. Open and emotionally grounded. Vulnerable and emotionally safe to love.

You're not too much, you just need more tools. And now you have them.

CRYSTAL CARMEN REAL TALK

- Feel everything, but don't weaponize it.

- Your tone, timing, and delivery matter more than you think.

- Don't just vent. Communicate. Don't collapse. Express.

- You can be emotional and emotionally intelligent, at the same damn time.

- If you want love, learn to be a safe space for it.

Journal Prompt

When I feel triggered, what is my typical response, and where did I learn it from?

What emotions do I avoid or suppress, and why?'

How can I express my needs without blame or emotional dumping?

What would it look like to respond with grace, even when I feel frustrated?

What new language can I practice using when I feel hurt, unseen, or overwhelmed?

The Power of Body Language: Femininity Without Saying a Word

Because a well-placed look can say more than a 30-minute convo.

Let's be real before anyone hears your voice, they've already read your energy. Your walk, your eye contact, the way you enter a room, that's the first impression. Not your words. Not your resume. Not even your waist-to-hip ratio.

Body language is your silent signature. And the good news? You can master it.

This chapter is about learning to speak volumes with a glance, a smile, a slow sip of wine, or the way you tilt your head when someone's wasting your time. It's about commanding attention without begging for it. It's about becoming unforgettable, before you even say hello.

POSTURE & POISE

Let's start with the basics: posture is power.

You want to instantly elevate your presence? Straighten your back. Roll those shoulders down. Chin up, not in arrogance, but in awareness.

You don't slump when you know you're the prize. And you sure as hell don't shrink to make others comfortable.

Poise isn't stiff, it's still. It's controlled. It's intentional. That calm, slow, deliberate grace? That's what feminine confidence looks like.

Practice walking like the floor is lucky to feel your heels. Because it is.

GESTURES & EXPRESSIVE HANDS

Your hands tell stories. They reveal nerves, confidence, ease, or tension. Feminine hand gestures are soft, fluid, and expressive without being frantic.

Don't overdo it. Don't fidget. Let your hands support your words like the backup dancers they are, not the lead singer.

Rest your hand lightly on your chest when making a point. Touch your collarbone when expressing warmth. Gently touch his arm to emphasize connection.

And when in doubt? Slow. It. Down.

There's nothing feminine about frantic energy. Stillness is seductive.

EYE CONTACT & FACIAL EXPRESSIONS

You ever give a man a look across the room and he just knows? That's the power of eye contact.

Strong eye contact says, I see you. But soft, intentional eye contact says, You can approach.

Let your eyes speak before your mouth ever does. Feminine eye contact is warm, inviting, and full of curiosity, but it's also sharp enough to slice through nonsense.

And don't forget the micro-expressions: a slight smile, a raised brow, a slow blink. These are the details that create chemistry without saying a damn word.

SMILING WITH RADIANCE

Your smile is your superpower. But not the fake, customer-service one. I'm talking about the real one, the one that starts in your eyes, melts into your lips, and lights up your whole aura.

Smile because you know you're radiant. Smile because you're in your joy. Smile because it makes you magnetic.

You don't have to force it. A soft smirk can be just as powerful as a bright grin when it's authentic.

Feminine energy doesn't perform, it shines.

VOCAL TONE & MODULATION

Let's talk about your voice, because how you speak matters as much as what you say.

A feminine voice doesn't have to be whispery or high-pitched. It just needs to be intentional. Use pauses. Let your words linger. Drop your tone slightly when making a point. It creates gravity.

Think velvet, not sandpaper.

And if you tend to rush when you're nervous? Practice slowing your speech. Confidence lives in the pause.

DRESSING TO COMPLEMENT YOUR BODY LANGUAGE

Clothing is a part of your body language, it tells the room how to treat you before you say a word.

You don't have to wear tight clothes or show skin to be feminine. But your clothes should reflect the energy you want to embody.

Soft fabrics, intentional fits, colors that make your skin glow, this is how you dress in harmony with your message.

Wear what makes you feel like HER.

Because when you feel sensual, powerful, and grounded in your look? The room feels it too.

PERSONAL SPACE & TOUCH

Feminine energy knows how to hold space, and how to protect it.

Don't crowd people. Don't chase attention. Let others come to you.

And when it comes to touch? Less is more.

A light graze on the arm. A gentle touch on the hand when laughing. A slow lean-in when someone is speaking. These moments of intentional touch say, I'm here. I'm connected. And they leave a lasting imprint.

Just like a great perfume, you want to linger, not overwhelm.

Your body is always talking. The question is: Are you in control of what it's saying?

When you master body language, you don't need to overshare, over- talk, or overprove. You just are. And people feel that before they even know your name.

Start moving like a woman who knows she's the moment. Because you are.

CRYSTAL CARMEN REAL TALK

- Your body speaks louder than your words, train it to tell the truth you want the world to know.

- Grace is power. Stillness is seductive. Movement is a message.

- Eye contact and posture can land you more dates,   more respect,   and better energy than any bio ever will.

- Dress like your energy deserves to be worshipped. Because it does.

- Don't chase the room. Command it, with silence, stillness, and presence.

JOURNAL PROMPTS

What is my body language saying about me before I speak?

Do I rush, fidget, or shrink when I'm unsure, and how can I shift that?

What colors, fabrics,   and fits make me feel my most radiant and feminine?

Where do I need to slow down in movement, speech, or presence?

THE ART OF FLIRTING

C aptivate and Charm with Grace

Because you don't chase, you attract. And baby, your energy enters the room before you do.

Flirting isn't desperation. It's not manipulation. And it's definitely not about throwing yourself at someone hoping they'll see your worth.

Flirting is a feminine superpower. It's the spark. The game before the game. The art of intrigue, mystery, and knowing exactly how to drop breadcrumbs without serving the whole damn cake.

This chapter is your permission to be playful. To captivate without clinging. To charm without shrinking. Because the right kind of flirting isn't about impressing a man, it's about inspiring one.

Let's get into it.

UNDERSTANDING THE ESSENCE OF FLIRTING

Flirting is emotional foreplay. It's how you create a vibe, an energy, an invitation for someone to approach, engage, and earn your attention.

It's not forced. It's flow.

It's the way your eyes linger, the way your voice softens, the way you giggle, not because he's hilarious, but because you're enjoying yourself.

Flirting is feminine energy in motion. Playful. Receptive. Irresistible.

SELF-CONFIDENCE & APPROACHABILITY

Let's get one thing clear: confidence is the foundation of good flirting.

But not the loud, performative kind. I'm talking about the kind of confidence that says, I like me. A lot. And you'd be lucky to get to know me.

Approachability doesn't mean being overly available. It means your energy says, "You may, " instead of "Don't you dare."

Make eye contact. Smile. Let your body language open up. And most importantly, flirt because you're enjoying the moment, not because you're trying to catch someone.

THE ART OF PLAYFUL BANTER

You don't need to be a comedian to be charming. Just light. Playful. Unbothered.

Tease him a little. Be witty. Raise your eyebrow and let your smile say, "I'm not easily impressed, but I'm intrigued."

Keep it fun, not forced. Leave space for pauses. And if the conversation doesn't naturally flow? You're allowed to bow out gracefully. That's flirting too.

Crystal's Confession

There's nothing sexier than a woman who flirts for her own pleasure.

Not because she's desperate. Not because she needs attention. But because she's in her fun, soft, magnetic energy. That's when it becomes art.

I've flirted with a man I had zero romantic interest in, just because I was feeling myself that day. It wasn't about him. It was about me enjoying my own vibe.

And that? That's the kind of confidence that turns heads without lifting a finger.

ACTIVE LISTENING & GENUINE INTEREST

Want to really stand out? Listen.

Ask questions. React to what he says. Mirror his tone lightly. Show him that you're present, not just playing a role.

Men are used to being ignored while women talk about themselves. A woman who listens with warmth and curiosity? Rare. Memorable. Irresistible.

Flirting isn't about convincing someone they're amazing. It's about noticing something unique and reflecting it back in a way that feels intentional.

Say it like this:

- "You have that 'calm but dangerous' energy."

- "I like your style. You pay attention to details."

- "There's something about your voice. It's grounding."

Flatter lightly and with style. Never beg. Never oversell. You're a luxury item, not a clearance bin.

CREATING MYSTERY & INTRIGUE

Here's a secret: you don't have to tell him everything.

In fact, the less you say, the more he'll wonder. You're not hiding, you're just letting the story unfold.

Talk about your passions, not your problems. Share hints, not a full timeline. Let your mystery simmer. Flirting is foreplay, and good foreplay teases without rushing.

Crystal's Confessions

At one point, a long time ago, I thought overly flirty banter was a good way to show a guy I liked him. I thought being playful and light with innuendos made me seem fun and sexy.

But here's what I learned: they mistook it for sexual interest only.

Suddenly the conversations would shift. The vibe would change. And what started as fun turned into disrespect.

So I leveled up.

I learned to observe. To choose my words with intention. To not tolerate inappropriate jokes or sexualized conversations that didn't align with the energy I wanted.

It was a game changer. I started having only high-vibrational conversations, with men who were respectful, thoughtful, and kind.

And guess what? Men liked this. Even the ones I declined interest in found it alluring that I had boundaries. Some even circled back later and apologized for how they initially came at me.

That's when I understood: protecting your energy is seductive. And flirting doesn't mean sacrificing your standards.

HANDLING REJECTION WITH GRACE

Not every flirt turns into a date, and that's okay.

You're not for everyone. You're for the right one. If someone doesn't respond or reciprocate, that's a gift. You've just been redirected. Gracefully.

Confidence is knowing your energy is gold whether someone fumbles it or not.

KNOW WHAT YOU'RE SIGNALING

Let's also be clear about this: if you want a man who is a leader, protector, and provider, he will pursue you. That's how real masculine energy operates. So stop thinking you need to perform to get picked.

There's nothing wrong with a coy smile. A soft laugh. A flirty glance. That's feminine mystery. That's magnetic.

But throwing yourself at him? Talking about sex too soon? Being overly aggressive or overexposed? That might get his attention... but not in the way you want.

Don't confuse desire with devotion. You're not here to be a thrill. You're here to be a woman worth choosing, keeping, and protecting.

FLIRTING IN THE DIGITAL AGE

Yes, you can flirt through text. The same rules apply: keep it light, keep it teasing, keep it mysterious.

Use emojis sparingly. Send voice notes if you want to stand out. And please, no paragraph-long life stories in the DMs. Save the soul for the slow drip.

FLIRTING ACROSS CULTURES & CONTEXTS

Read the room. What's flirty in Philly may be too forward in Paris.

Stay intuitive. Be aware of energy. Adjust your approach without changing who you are. Feminine energy travels well when it's laced with respect and curiosity.

Flirting is an art. It's the sprinkle of glitter, not the whole costume. It's charm without attachment. Playfulness without pressure.

You are not auditioning. You're inviting. You're showing someone a glimpse of your light, and letting them work to see more.

So soften your eyes. Tilt your head. Let your laugh linger. And know that the real seduction? Is in your energy.

CRYSTAL CARMEN REAL TALK

- Flirting is play, not performance. Keep it light, not needy.

- Your energy does the work, your words are just the accessories.

- Confidence is your best pickup line.

- You don't have to reveal everything to make a connection.

- Flirt for you, not for validation.

JOURNAL PROMPTS

When was the last time I flirted just for fun, and how did it feel?

What makes me feel playful, magnetic, and flirtatious?

Do I overshare too soon in new connections? How can I create more mystery?

What are 3 compliments I can use that feel natural to my personality?

What would it look like to flirt with life, not just people?

SETTING BOUNDARIES WITH ELEGANCE

B ecause a soft "no" in the right tone can protect your peace better than a loud breakdown ever could.

Let's start with the truth:

You're not "mean" for setting boundaries. You're just finally respecting your own energy.

A high-value woman doesn't let everyone in. She doesn't explain her standards 12 times. She doesn't apologize for knowing what she needs and what she refuses to tolerate.

Boundaries are not walls. They're doors, with locks, keys, and instructions for how you may enter.

And when you learn how to set them with elegance?

You stop attracting confusion. You start commanding clarity.

WHAT BOUNDARIES REALLY ARE

Boundaries aren't ultimatums.

They're not about control.

They're about clarity.

Boundaries are how you teach people to treat you. They are the lines between what supports your peace, and what sabotages it.

- "Please don't raise your voice when we talk."

- "I'm not comfortable sharing that detail right now."

- "I'm not available for last-minute plans."

Simple. Clear. Direct. And yes, still feminine.

Crystal's Confession

When I really started honoring my boundaries, I began to notice something...How few women actually do.

I saw it everywhere, women apologizing for no reason, starting their sentences with "I just..." to minimize themselves, and accepting the bare minimum because a man said one thing... while showing them another.

Let me be real with you:

You will be affected and respected based on what you tolerate.

And to be honest? I'm not even chasing anyone's respect.

What I am making clear is that I'm not here for lies, cheating, exaggeration, or men flaunting money to distract from their character.

You can have a bag and still be bankrupt morally.

I like a man whose character and how he moves tells me everything I need to know.

Don't get fooled by money when the morals are missing.

SETTING BOUNDARIES ISN'T RUDENESS, IT'S REFINEMENT

You don't have to scream to be taken seriously.

You don't have to cut someone off to create space.

You don't have to be cold to be clear.

Elegant boundaries are quiet, firm, and backed by action.

- You don't keep explaining the same thing.

- You don't keep forgiving the same disrespect.

- You don't stay where your peace is constantly being tested.

Boundaries don't always sound like "no."

Sometimes they sound like silence. Like leaving. Like not answering the phone after the third broken promise.

BOUNDARIES START AT HOME

Let's talk truth:

Boundaries don't just apply in romantic relationships. They start with your family.

And if we're being honest, a lot of us were taught to ignore our boundaries before we ever started dating.

See, there's a difference between being told what to do for your own good, when you're a child, still learning, still developing, and being told what to do because someone wants to control every aspect of who you are.

That second one? That's not parenting.

That's programming.

My dad, for example, was notorious for pushing people's boundaries. He'd try to make you taste something you didn't want, or tell you how you should feel, as if your no didn't matter.

And when that kind of behavior comes from someone you love and trust? You start associating love with discomfort.

Control starts to feel normal.

Being overruled starts to feel like "care."

So as an adult, when someone disrespects you, you tolerate it, because it feels familiar.

But here's what I had to learn:

Even family doesn't get to override your peace.

You can love them. You can honor them.

And still say, "That doesn't work for me anymore."

That's not rebellion. That's reprogramming.

Boundaries in Romantic Relationships

This is where it gets juicy.

You want a man to lead? Then let him step up, but you still get to choose where the line is.

You can be soft and still say:

- "That joke isn't funny to me."

- "If we're not exclusive, I'm not investing emotionally."

- "I'm not interested in situationships. I date with intention."

Boundaries tell a man how to treat you.

If he's high-quality, he won't feel offended, he'll feel guided.

If he's low-quality, he'll either test them or disappear. Either way, you win.

Non-Negotiables: Clear Without the Checklist

Non-negotiables don't have to be announced like you're running HR for your love life. They show up gradually, in conversation, in how you live, and in what you allow. The point is that you are very clear on what you want and what you don't, and anything that doesn't match that has no room to grow.

With Ryan, it became clear early on. I don't do 50-50. I've tried it it but I wasn't raised in it and doesn't feel good. I don't do trash. I don't do windows. I don't do men with no sexual self-control. And I don't do endless girlfriend auditions when I know I'm a wife. If marriage isn't on the horizon, then I'm not your match.

These things weren't barked out like a list of rules. They came out naturally, in conversation, in the way I carried myself, in the standards I upheld. And guess what? The wrong men quietly exited. The right one leaned in.

I've also had the other side of it   where I could tell a man was interested, maybe even thought about taking things to the next level. But he wasn't serious. He was just hanging on because of proximity and comfort. That's not my vibe. Either you're all in, or you're all out. Half-love and half-commitment are no love at all.

Because here's the truth: when you know your non-negotiables, you don't need to scream them. You live them. And the men who are meant for you will either rise to meet them or fade themselves out.

Crystal Carmen Real Talk: Key Takeaways

Non-negotiables are lived, not barked out.

Clarity doesn't scare the right man, it attracts him.

A half-commitment is no commitment.

Proximity is not love , don't confuse comfort with investment.

When you know your non-negotiables, you protect your peace before you ever have to defend it.

DEALING WITH PUSHBACK

Listen, people who benefitted from your lack of boundaries will absolutely be uncomfortable when you start setting them.

Let them be.

You're not responsible for their reaction. You're responsible for your standards.

They'll say:

- "You've changed."

- "You're too much now."

- "Why are you being difficult?"

Here's what you say:

"I'm being clear."

Let them sit with that.

People who can't respect your boundaries are those want to benefit from you not having them.

GRACEFUL WAYS TO SAY "NO"

Here are some elegant phrases you can start using today:

- "That doesn't work for me, but I appreciate the offer."

- "I need a little time before I can say yes to that."

- "That's not aligned with my priorities right now."

- "I'm unavailable for that type of dynamic."

- "That's not something I choose to participate in."

No attitude. No mess. Just clarity and class.

BOUNDARIES AS SELF-CARE

Every time you honor your boundaries, you tell your nervous system:

"I got you."

That's real self-care.

Not just spa days, but safety.

Not just journaling, but decisions that protect your peace and energy.

Boundaries are how you parent your inner child.

They're how you break cycles your mother didn't know how to break.

They're how you create love that doesn't leave you depleted.

Let me tell you how I used to handle boundaries...

Someone would push the envelope, make a slick comment, say something inappropriate, do something that made me feel uncomfortable. And when I finally said something?

They'd hit me with a half-hearted apology.

And I'd let it go.

Because I didn't want to be "too much."

Because I didn't want to make things awkward.

Because I wanted to be seen as understanding.

You know what happened 100% of the time?

They did it again.

That's when I realized, boundaries without reinforcement are just suggestions.

Now? I check it once. Clearly.

And if they don't shift?

Get to steppin'.

I'm not repeating myself for grown folks. I'm not shrinking my standards to keep the peace. Because every time you let it slide, you teach them how far they can go.

You can be soft.

You can be sensual.

You can be radiant and deeply feminine.

And still say "no" like a woman who means it.

Setting boundaries with elegance doesn't make you difficult. It makes you divine.

You don't just teach people how to treat you, you teach them how to value you.

And when you set the standard?

Only the ones who rise to meet it stay.

CRYSTAL CARMEN REAL TALK

- Boundaries are not walls, they are doors with standards.

- You are not rude for protecting your peace.

- The more you tolerate, the less you're respected.

- Boundaries can be soft, but they should always be firm.

- The man who wants to love you well will honor your boundaries, not run from them.

JOURNAL PROMPTS

Where in my life am I currently tolerating something that drains me?

What boundary do I need to reinforce, with love and firmness?

What makes me feel guilty about saying no? Where did that belief come from?

How do I want to be treated, and have I communicated that clearly?

What is one boundary I can set this week that protects my peace?

What are your top five non-negotiables in a relationship? Write them down clearly.

How do you want these to show up in your conversations and actions naturally, not as ultimatums?

Have you ever bent or ignored your own non-negotiables? What happened, and how did it make you feel?

Imagine the next man you date respects all of your non-negotiables. How would that change the way you move in the relationship?

EMBRACING VULNERABILITY

B ecause the love you want can't find you behind the wall you built to survive.

Vulnerability is not weakness.

Let's say that again for the girls in the back: Vulnerability is not weakness.

It is the most courageous act of femininity. It is how you open your heart without fear of being swallowed. It is how you create real intimacy, not just romance, but emotional closeness, spiritual safety, and genuine connection.

But for many of us, vulnerability is scary because we were trained to believe it made us a target.

And if you've ever lived through betrayal, abuse, emotional abandonment, or unhealed heartbreak... you probably learned how to survive by hiding the softest parts of yourself.

This chapter is about unlearning that survival script.

It's about reclaiming the beauty and strength in being open.

Because if you want deep love,you have to show up as the real you.

THE COST OF ARMOR

Being "strong" isn't always about lifting weight. Sometimes, it's about carrying trauma and calling it independence.

A lot of women walk into relationships armored up, emotionally unavailable, and guarded, then wonder why they only attract surface-level connections or emotionally immature men.

Here's the truth:

You cannot attract true intimacy if you're afraid to be seen.

And yes,there's a difference between discernment and emotional lockdown.

Crystal's Confession

Over time, I realized vulnerability was frightening for me. When I was young, I had an abusive dad. I just wanted love. I wanted to be open. But I'd be so shocked when he'd turn on me for no reason,when he was angry or drunk. I learned quickly: love wasn't safe, and being open made me a target.

So I became harder. More rigid. I swallowed my feelings.

I "manned up." I tried to become someone he couldn't hurt anymore.

And that mindset followed me into adulthood.

I lived in masculine energy. I had my walls all the way up. And when it came to dating, it was like watching two dudes trying to date, because here I was, trying to lead, compete, control, and protect. Vulnerability felt like a setup.

I used to look at my mom, so soft, so loving, always cooking for my dad, taking care of him... and I'd think: Why? He doesn't even see it. He doesn't honor it.

But then something shifted.

I realized that vulnerability isn't about being walked on.

It's about being authentic.

It's about letting someone see you so fully that there's no performance left.

And now? I know that when I'm vulnerable in the right space,with a man who cherishes me,it's not dangerous. It's divine. I can cry, I can be held, I can ask for what I need without shame. And he doesn't see me as less. He sees me as real.

Vulnerability also shows up in friendships.

Just recently, I told one of my closest friends something raw and real:

"Are you kidding me? I couldn't even imagine this wedding happening without you here."

That was vulnerability. That was me exposing my heart.

And she showed up.

If I hadn't been willing to speak my truth... I would've missed that moment.

That's the beauty of vulnerability. It lets love all the way in.

Crystal's Confession

Let me tell you something about Ryan

My husband,

I love this man. Truly. Deeply.

But I need you to hear me when I say:

Loving him has required a new kind of strength.

Not the kind I used to rely on, the hyper-independent, armor-up, "I got it" strength.

No.

This time, I had to be strong enough to trust.

Strong enough to soften.

Strong enough to be seen.

It's one thing to fall in love.

It's another to stay soft in the presence of someone who sees all of you.

I've had to be strong enough to show my tears, my fears, my insecurities.

To trust that he wouldn't flinch. To believe that he could hold it all without judging me, abandoning me, or using my softness against me.

And let me tell you something:

He has. Unwavering. Patience for me. Steady. Every single time.

Loving him has shown me that real love doesn't require you to dim or hide.

It asks you to be real, and rewards you for it.

So to every woman scared to take the armor off:

The right man doesn't just handle your vulnerability, he honors it.

WHAT VULNERABILITY REALLY IS

Vulnerability is not trauma dumping.

It's not telling your life story on the second date.

It's not asking someone to hold emotions they haven't earned the right to see.

Vulnerability is:

- Saying "I miss you" without needing a response

- Admitting, "That hurt my feelings" instead of acting like it didn't

- Letting your voice shake while still speaking your truth

- Saying "I need support" instead of pretending you're fine

Vulnerability doesn't beg,it reveals.
And it only reveals to safe spaces.

SOFTNESS IS STRATEGY

You don't have to lead every conversation.
You don't have to have all the answers.
You don't have to perform to prove your worth.
Sometimes, being vulnerable is letting silence speak for you.
It's allowing yourself to feel without rushing to fix it.
It's letting someone be there,for real,for you.
The softness you've been scared to show?
That's the exact softness a healthy man is looking for.

BUILDING EMOTIONAL INTIMACY

Intimacy is not built through sex.
It's built through vulnerability.
The late-night conversation where you finally say, "Here's what I've been scared to tell you..."
The moment you let yourself cry in front of him and he doesn't flinch.
The time you let go of your "strong woman" mask and say, "I just want to feel safe."
That's intimacy. That's connection.
And that's what opens the door to true, soul-level love.

IF YOU WERE TAUGHT THAT VULNERABILITY IS WEAKNESS

Unlearn it.

Challenge it.

Break up with the version of you that only knows how to protect herself with pride, pain, and perfectionism.

Because true healing comes when you realize:

You are safest when you're seen fully by someone who chooses you anyway.

Being vulnerable doesn't mean you're broken. It means you're brave.

It means you are done hiding behind filters, attitudes, and emotional detachment.

It means you are choosing real intimacy, even if it feels scary.

And when you embrace vulnerability as a feminine strength?

You attract people who don't just want you... they're ready to hold all of you.

Soft is not weak.

Soft is sacred.

Soft is strong.

CRYSTAL CARMEN REAL TALK

- Vulnerability is not weakness, it's emotional and mental strength.

- You cannot build intimacy while hiding your authentic self.

- The walls you built to protect yourself are blocking your blessings.

- When you choose vulnerability, you invite in connection.

- The right people will never make you feel unsafe for being real.

JOURNAL PROMPTS

What parts of myself do I keep hidden, and why?

Who in my life feels emotionally safe to be vulnerable with?

What did I learn about vulnerability growing up?

When was a time I showed vulnerability and it created deeper love?

What is one way I can practice softness this week without fear?

Communication: Expressing Needs and Desires in a Feminine Approach

B ecause the way you say it is just as important as what you say.

Let's be clear, feminine energy doesn't mean silence.

It means being intentional, intuitive, and emotionally intelligent with your words.

You don't have to scream, argue, or demand to get what you need.

You don't have to talk in circles or dim yourself to keep the peace.

You can ask. You can express. You can clarify your expectations...

With softness. With clarity. With power.

And that is the secret to getting your needs met without losing your femininity.

THE POWER OF FEMININE COMMUNICATION

Feminine communication is rooted in connection, not control.

It's about expression, not dominance.

It's not "talking less", it's knowing when, why, and how to speak.

A high-value woman speaks life, not confusion.

She knows her voice is sacred. She uses it to create safety, not chaos.

TONE > WORDS

Let's talk about it:

Your tone is the message before your message.

You can say "we need to talk" and create dread, or you can say,

"Hey love, can I share something with you when you have space?"

Same topic. Different energy.

Your feminine communication is in:

- Your timing

- Your tone

- Your body language

- Your energy

Men, especially providers and protectors, respond to softness not weakness, grace not passivity, and clarity not complaints.

Crystal's Confession

TIMING IS EVERYTHING

There was a time I used to bring things up in the heat of my emotions.

He'd be drained, I'd be frustrated, and I'd jump right in:

"Why haven't you...?" "We need to talk..." "You always..."

What I didn't realize was... I wasn't creating connection, I was creating resistance.

When you're emotionally triggered, it's easy to make your needs sound like demands.

But emotional intelligence taught me this:

The "when" is just as powerful as the "what."

Now I approach hard conversations with intention. I watch the moment, I mind my tone, and I speak from a place of peace, not pressure.

And guess what?

He listens. Every time.

COMMUNICATING NEEDS VS. MAKING DEMANDS

You are allowed to want what you want.

You are allowed to express your desires.

But it's not about barking orders, it's about inviting partnership.

Instead of:

- "You never help around the house."

Try:

- "It would really make me feel supported if we handled this together."

Instead of:

- "You don't even care."

Try:

- "When that happens, I feel disconnected, and I really value our closeness."

Feminine communication never ignores the truth, it just delivers it with intention, not injury.

DON'T TRAUMA DUMP, TRUST BUILD

Emotional honesty is not a greenlight for emotional dumping.

You don't need to tell someone everything all at once.

You don't need to use communication as a test to see if they'll stay.

That's not expression. That's fear dressed up as sharing.

True feminine expression comes from a place of calm confidence:

- "This is what I need."

- "This is how I feel."

- "This is what works for me."

- "This is what I'm choosing moving forward."

Clear. Elegant. Empowered.

FEMININE ASSERTIVENESS IS A GIFT

You can say no without being harsh.

You can speak up without yelling.

You can ask for more without begging.

Here are some examples:

- "That's not in alignment with me."

- "I need some time to think about that."

- "I'd love to do that, but here's what I need first."

- "I'm not available for that, but I wish you well."

That's not passive. That's poised.

A HIGH-VALUE, WOMAN COMMUNICATES WITH INTENTION

She doesn't overshare with the wrong people.

She doesn't shrink or over-explain.

She speaks with purpose.

And when she speaks, you listen. Because her energy is grounded, her mind is clear, and her words are meant.

IF YOU WANT TO BE LED, YOU HAVE TO LET HIM HEAR YOU

Here's the secret sauce:

Men who are leaders want to meet your needs, but they're not mind readers.

If you don't express yourself, you end up:

- Resentful

- Misunderstood

- Or worst... passive-aggressively testing him

Speak your truth. Ask for clarity.

Then lean back and observe.

The right man listens. The wrong man gets defensive.

That alone tells you what you need to know.

Crystal's Confession

DON'T MATCH HIS ANGER, MASTER YOUR OWN ENERGY

Something I had to learn the hard way?

Don't match his anger. Don't mirror his defensiveness.

Sometimes, when a man is triggered, especially around topics like money, decisions, or leadership, it's not because you're wrong. It's because he feels exposed.

Men aren't always taught how to process truth.

They're taught to lead, to provide, to protect, so when you speak something that makes them feel like they're failing in those roles?

It lands like a wound, not wisdom.

I remember how uncomfortable conversations about spending used to be with my husband.

At first, he'd get frustrated. Defensive. Short.

But here's the truth:

He always wanted to make sure I could go on any date I wanted. He took so much pride in making me happy.

And I noticed it might've been affecting his budget, but he would never say it.

So I brought it up, not from a place of criticism, but from care.

Because this wasn't some casual situation. This was my future husband.

And I wasn't trying to judge him, I was trying to make sure we were in sync.

At first, he didn't know how to take it.

But I stayed calm. I stayed loving. I didn't match the tension, I held space.

And over time, he saw it.

He understood I wasn't trying to shame him, I was trying to build with him.

I wasn't asking for control, I was asking for alignment.

That's what feminine communication is:

It's saying the truth, without cutting someone with it.

And it works when you stay steady, even when they wobble.

Your voice is a feminine superpower.

Use it to build. Use it to inspire.

Use it to set the tone for the kind of love, peace, and respect you want.

Soft doesn't mean silent. Clear doesn't mean cruel.

And honest doesn't mean hostile.

Say what you mean. Mean what you say. And say it with grace.

You don't have to pick: Power or peace. Strong or soft.

Independent or loved. You get to be both.

The woman who knows how to lead and lean back...

The woman who knows when to speak and when to smile...

The woman who can create her own table and be invited to one where she's cherished...

She is unstoppable.

Let the world see your fire.

But let your man feel your glow.

You can be a lover, a classy woman, a vixen, am other and a boss babe

Because baby, you are all of it.

And the real flex is knowing how to move through each role without losing yourself in any of them.

JOURNAL PROMPTS

Do I feel safe expressing my needs? Why or why not?

What tone or timing habit do I want to change in my communication?

How do I feel when my voice is truly heard and honored?

Who in my life brings out the best in my communication style?

How can I practice expressing one desire this week with softness and clarity?

Strength in Softness

B ecause you don't have to choose between being powerful and being soft. You can be both, and you should be.

Balancing Independence and Softness

Here's the lie we were sold:

You're either the boss chick... or the sweetheart.

You're either strong... or you're feminine.

You're either independent... or you need someone.

False.

A high-value woman knows how to move with grace and grit.

She can take care of herself and let a man lead.

She can speak her mind and still be soft.

She's the whole package, because she knows she doesn't have to shrink one part to make the other shine.

This chapter is for the woman who's tired of being told she's too much, too strong, too successful, too opinionated, and is ready to show that her gentleness is where her true power lives.

WHY WE BUILD ARMOR

Let's be honest, most of us didn't become hyper-independent for fun.

We became independent because we had to.

Because no one else was going to do it.

Because being "too soft" left us unprotected.

Because the people we were supposed to rely on... disappointed us.

So we took over.

Paid our own bills.

Fixed our own cars.

Built businesses. Raised babies. Created our own peace.

And let's be clear, there's no shame in that.

But eventually, the very thing that helped us survive... starts getting in the way of what we actually want:

- To be cared for

- To feel held

- To be in a partnership that feels like home

The truth is... we don't want to be hard.

We just want to feel safe enough to be soft.

STRENGTH IN SOFTNESS

Soft doesn't mean silent.

Soft doesn't mean weak.

Soft means choosing grace when ego wants to scream.

Soft means trusting your intuition instead of trying to control everything.

It takes real strength to:

- Let someone in

- Receive help

- Trust a man to lead

- Speak gently when you've been trained to defend

That's divine feminine energy.

It's not submissive, it's magnetic.

Crystal's Confession

WHEN I USED TO ACT LIKE THE MAN I WANTED

Let me be real with you.

There was a time when I moved like the man I wanted to marry.

I was leading the conversation, making the plans, handling the finances, and checking in on his emotional state.

It was giving... masculine overload.

And I couldn't figure out why I kept attracting men who wanted to be taken care of, but never wanted to take the lead.

Then I had to face it:

I was auditioning for the CEO of the relationship.

So that's who I kept attracting, interns.

The truth is, I didn't trust anyone to lead me, love me, or protect me... so I kept trying to do both roles.

And that energy?

It was exhausting.

But once I started balancing my power with peace, my independence with softness, and my strength with surrender, everything shifted.

I stopped dating projects.

I started attracting providers.

I stopped leading every conversation.

I started receiving.

Softness didn't cost me anything.

It added everything.

YOU DON'T HAVE TO CHOOSE, YOU JUST HAVE TO ALIGN

You can be a boss.

You can make six figures.

You can run your business, pay your bills, and still say:

- "I love when you handle that."

- "I trust your decision."

- "Thank you for taking care of that for us."

- "I feel so safe when you lead."

That doesn't make you weak. That makes you wise.

It's not about dependence.

It's about mutual fulfillment.

Because here's what I know:

A strong woman who chooses softness will always win.

WHAT GENTLENESS LOOKS LIKE

- Saying "no" without the need to explain or over-apologize

- Letting a man take the lead without feeling like you've lost yourself

- Speaking your truth without raising your voice

- Resting in your femininity without guilt

You don't need to be hard to be taken seriously.

You don't need to fight to be valued.

You need to flow with discernment, not force.

When you're used to being in control, receiving feels uncomfortable.

But receiving is where the magic happens.

It says: "I trust life. I trust love. I trust myself enough to open."

Stop blocking your blessings by trying to do everything.

Let him carry that bag.

Let him plan the date.

Let him show up for you.

Being soft enough to receive isn't lazy, it's luxury energy.

You don't have to pick:

Power or peace.

Strong or soft.

Independent or loved.

You get to be both.

The woman who knows how to lead and lean back...

The woman who knows when to speak and when to smile...

The woman who can create her own table and be invited to one where she's cherished...

She is unstoppable.

Let the world see your fire.

But let your man feel your glow.

And in the words of that classic song,

"I'm a bitch, I'm a lover, I'm a child, I'm a mother... I'm a sinner, I'm a saint, I do not feel ashamed."

Because baby, you are all of it.

And the real flex is knowing how to move through each role without losing yourself in any of them.

CRYSTAL UNFILTERED: FK* THE BOX

People will tell you:

"You have to be this way."

"You need to act like that."

They'll try to squeeze you into their little box because it makes them more comfortable.

Well baby, fk the box.

I like a little bit of country.

I'm also a little bit of rock 'n' roll.

I'm also like a modern day goth, I have more black clothes and chain accessories than I know what to do with.

But I also have bold, loud, wild colors.

And on any given Sunday, I can show up in all three.

And guess what?

My man will match my outfit AND my energy.

Because I'm not bending who I am to make anyone more comfortable.

And I'm damn sure not watering myself down just to be "more palatable."

People love to say:

"Oh, you're a hustler."

You're right. But let me be clear,

If you're going to call me a hustler,

Call me a hustler of hope.

Tell people I hustle women out of survival mode...

Out of broken systems and cycles...

And into lives they don't have to run from.

I hustle people into their power.

I hustle them into beauty, joy, healing, and clarity.

So say it loud.

Say it right.

I'm not hustling people, I'm helping them come home to themselves.

With love. With strategy. With softness. With truth.

And if that bothers you?

Well then, again...

Fk off.

Respectfully.

CRYSTAL CARMEN REAL TALK

- Softness is not weakness, it's spiritual strength

- Hyper-independence is often rooted in trauma, not truth

- You can be powerful and feminine, you don't have to pick one

- The energy you lead with determines who you attract

- Receiving is a sacred act of trust, not laziness or neediness

JOURNAL PROMPTS

Where in my life am I still leading from survival instead of softness?

What beliefs do I hold about being "too independent"?

When do I feel most safe to be soft?

How can I invite more gentleness into my day-to-day energy?

What would it feel like to be deeply supported, and am I open to it?

THE POWER IN BEING LED

F inding Freedom in Surrender

There is nothing weak about being led. In fact, it takes strength, confidence, and self-awareness to soften enough to let a man step into his role. Too many women hear the phrase "being led" and instantly think it means being powerless. They imagine control, dominance, or submission in the worst sense of the word. But here is the truth: when the right man leads, it feels like peace.

Being led is not about losing your voice. It is about gaining relief. It is the sweet exhale after holding your breath too long. It is the freedom of not having to do it all.

The Luxury of Leadership

I am a boss babe. I manage businesses, run a spa, write books, coach women, and raise children. My days are stacked with decisions. What client goes where. What supplier to use. What bill is due. What's for dinner. What event needs planning. Everyone and everything requires me to show up, decide, and deliver.

So when my husband comes home and says, "Hey, I got out of work early so I figured I'd take care of the laundry," it means more than clothes getting folded. It means I get to set one responsibility down. It means I can walk into my room and breathe. That is leadership. That is a man noticing where he can lighten my load without waiting to be told.

Being led by a high-value man is like slipping into silk after a long day in shapewear. You didn't even realize how tight everything was until suddenly you're comfortable again.

Wanting Love ≠ Centering Men

Somewhere along the way, women got told that wanting love means centering men. That is a lie.

There is a difference between desiring a healthy, intentional relationship and building your whole identity around a man. Wanting companionship does not erase your independence. It does not take away from your success, your ambition, or your purpose.

What it does is add balance. Having a man who can lead does not cancel who you are. It enhances who you are. It gives you space to rest.

The Walls We Build

The older we get, the harder it can be to let someone lead. I have heard women say, "Maybe God doesn't want me to be with anyone" or "I am better off alone." Sometimes those words are rooted in truth. But many times, they are rooted in fear.

When you have been hurt, overlooked, or betrayed, it feels safer to say you do not need anybody. It feels safer to build walls. And yet, those same walls that keep out pain also block love.

Being led requires vulnerability. It requires trust. And as women, the older we get, the more tempting it is to protect ourselves by refusing to soften. But let me tell you this: real leadership from a man is not about control. It is about protection. And if you never allow yourself to experience it, you miss out on one of the deepest gifts love can bring.

Stop Knocking Him Down

Sometimes men stop trying because they get knocked down too much.

He might come home with a rice cooker because he overheard you mention one. But instead of being grateful, you complain that it is not the stainless steel version to match your kitchen. He might pick up pillows for the couch and you roll your eyes because the color does not match the sofa.

Do you know what happens when you keep doing that? He stops trying.

And then you'll sit back and complain that he never surprises you or never takes initiative. When in reality, he learned that no matter what he did, it was not good enough.

There are moments in relationships where the best thing you can do is shut up and say thank you. Gratitude goes further than perfection.

Knowing When to Speak Up

Now, that does not mean you never use your voice. Part of the power in being led is knowing when to be quiet and when to speak up.

For example, my husband bought me a dress. It was beautiful, and I was flattered, but I knew I would need shapewear to wear it comfortably. Shapewear is not my favorite. Still, I wore it, and everyone loved it. He loved it too. I received compliment after compliment. So when he bought me the same dress in another color, I smiled and wore it again.

But one evening, he asked me to wear it to an event and I couldn't hide the look on my face. I didn't want to put myself through the discomfort again. So I told him. The conversation was not easy, but it was honest. His response was simple: "That's fine, wear it around the house for me."

That is balance. That is respect. Knowing when to quietly receive and when to lovingly express yourself is part of what makes being led work.

Client Story: When Gratitude Was Missing

I once had a client who complained constantly about her man. He cooked, he cleaned, he ran errands, but every effort was met with criticism. "He folded the towels wrong." "He didn't season the chicken the way I like." "He didn't plan the date exactly how I wanted."

Eventually, he stopped doing those things. Not because he didn't care, but because no effort was ever good enough. And the more he pulled away, the more she complained that he wasn't leading.

What she could not see was that she had created the very thing she feared. Gratitude is the fuel that keeps a man engaged. Without it, even the most intentional men will eventually check out.

Client Story: Fear of Losing Control

Another client of mine refused to let any man lead because she equated leadership with control. She grew up watching her mother submit to a toxic partner, so in her mind, letting a man lead meant losing herself.

When she came to me, she was exhausted from being in charge of everything. Her career. Her household. Her dating life. She complained that men she dated were passive, unmotivated, and uninspiring.

I had to tell her the truth: she was attracting passive men because she left no room for a man to lead. She made every decision before they could even offer. She created the dynamic she hated.

When she finally learned to soften, to allow space for a man to step in, everything changed. She attracted a man who was intentional, protective, and strong. And she realized that real leadership is not suffocating. It is safe.

Protection, Not Control

Let me make this clear: there is a difference between being controlled and being cared for.

A controlling man tells you what to do to limit you. A protective man leads you with intention so you can expand.

When my husband notices I am overworked and says, "Take a nap," he is not trying to shrink me. He is trying to restore me. I When he plans dinner, he is not taking away my role as a wife. He is showing me that I am worth being cared for.

Decades ago, I had to realize that my initial reaction is not always the right one. Someone telling me to take a nap back then would have me feel like I was being controlled inside. I would have tensed up and whether in my mind or out loud I would say "don't tell me what to do" but it was a trigger so it was subconscious and automatic. I had to learn to assume he has my best interest at heart, lets see what that feels like,

Being led by the right man does not silence your voice. It gives you the freedom to use it more intentionally.

The power in being led is about trust, safety, and balance. It is about knowing that you do not always have to carry everything. It is about learning when to receive instead of resist.

Strong women need this more than anyone. Boss babes, entrepreneurs, mothers, leaders. We are so used to carrying the weight that we forget the gift of being carried.

Letting a man lead is not weakness. It is wisdom. It is softness. It is love in action.

Crystal Carmen Real Talk

Being led by the right man feels like peace, not control.

Gratitude matters more than perfection. Stop knocking down his efforts.

Knowing when to soften and when to speak up creates balance.

Vulnerability gets harder with age, but it is worth the risk.

A man who leads with intention allows you to rest, not shrink.

Journal Prompts

Where in your life are you carrying more than you need to?

When was the last time you said "thank you" instead of offering criticism?

What fears come up for you when you think about letting someone else lead?

Can you recall a moment when someone's leadership allowed you to rest? How did it feel?

What specific areas would you like to practice receiving more in your current or future relationship?

Sensuality: Igniting Passion and Deepening Connection

B ecause your softness, your scent, your voice, your rhythm are sacred.

Let's clear something up right now:

Sensuality is not just about sex.

It's about aliveness.

It's how you experience life, how you move through a room, how you taste food, take in music, and touch your own skin.

It's how you receive.

It's how you respond.

It's how you radiate... without even trying.

And when a woman is tapped into her sensuality, not performance, not seduction, but true embodied sensuality?

She doesn't chase. She attracts.

This chapter is about waking that up.

WHAT SENSUALITY ACTUALLY IS

Sensuality is the language of the feminine.

It's not about pleasing others, it's about feeling good in your own skin.

It's:

- The way you moisturize your body after a shower

- The way you sip your tea slowly and actually taste it

- The way you walk across the room with hips that speak without saying a word

- The way you feel pleasure without apology

Sensuality says: I am home in my body. I trust my senses. I let beauty live here.

SOFTNESS THAT STAYS ON HIS MIND

Let's be honest, men remember how you make them feel.

Not just how you look.

But how you moved. How you touched. How you smelled. How you responded to life.

That soft "mmhmm" in a conversation.

That gentle brush of your hand.

The way you lean in with your eyes, not just your words.

Sensuality isn't loud. It lingers.

It's the whisper of your presence long after you've left the room.

Crystal's Confession

I used to be really clumsy, rushing everything, always in a hurry, trying to get to the next thing.

I didn't know how to be present.

I didn't know how to move slowly with intention.

But once I learned to slow down?

Everything changed.

I stopped tripping.

I stopped bumping into furniture and missing the beauty around me.

I became more graceful, not just in motion, but in how I received attention.

Men noticed.

And not because I changed my hair or makeup.

But because I started moving like I belonged in every room I walked into.

Grace is attractive.

Presence is powerful.

And intention? It's unforgettable.

HOW TO IGNITE SENSUAL ENERGY (WITHOUT FEELING OVEREXPOSED)

You don't have to bare it all to be sensual.

You don't have to be dripping in lingerie or pouting into the camera.

True sensuality is felt. Not forced.

Try this:

- Touch your neck when you speak to soften your voice

- Hold the stem of your wine glass like it's part of your outfit

- Let your laughter trail just a little longer

- Wear fragrances that remind you of love

- Add a touch that lingers, a gentle caress, a soft wave, and a flirty blush

It's not about being "on", it's about being in tune.

THE DIFFERENCE BETWEEN SENSUALITY & SEXUALIZATION

Let's get clear.

You can be sensual without inviting unwanted energy.

Sensuality is yours.

Sexualization is how others choose to perceive it.

The key is intention.

When your sensuality comes from confidence, it's magnetic.

When it comes from insecurity or people-pleasing, it becomes performative.

You're not sensual to get a man's attention.

You're sensual because it feels damn good to be connected to your body.

Crystal's Confession

MARRIED AND STILL MAGNETIC

Let me be clear, just because I'm married doesn't mean the romance is on autopilot.

I still seduce my husband.

I send him sexy photos, not porn, but definitely sensual. Just for his eyes.

Photos that say: I still want you. I still feel good in this body. I'm yours.

And you know what? That energy carries all day.

I wear his favorite perfume, just a little on the back of my neck and on my collarbone, so when he leans in to kiss me, it stays with him.

When I wake up, even before I check a single text, I center myself. I meditate.

And yes, I still make the effort to look good, because when I look good, I feel good.

It might be a pretty pajama set or just glowy, moisturized skin and a soft flush of color on my lips.

Not for the world.

For me. For him. For us.

And when I'm in the kitchen? Oh, it's a whole experience.

I make it a point to do a little something extra, whether it's how my hair is styled or how soft my skin feels, because I want him to see his beautiful wife using her love and safe energy to stir up a recipe...

that'll stir his loins later.

And let's not forget one of the most sacred parts of feminine care:

Your soft spot deserves luxury, too.

I use intimate washes that keep me fresh, soft, and balanced, like my foaming Bougie Garden wash.

It keeps me moisturized, delicious, and baby...

he can smell it.

Not just in the air.

When he leans in close, it hits him like a scent trail of temptation.

It reminds him, I washed her. She's fresh. And she's ready to be eaten like a mango.

That's the kind of intentional care that doesn't need a word.

It speaks for you.

And since we're being real?

Unsolicited oral sex is a whole love language.

There's something powerful about giving your man pleasure without him asking, without any strings, just because you want to.

It's not about submission in the patriarchal way, it's about giving him a moment where he gets to be desired, pampered, and spoiled.

When it's done with intention, genuine desire, and no pressure? It's healing. It's magnetic. It's unforgettable.

Because even the strongest man needs a space to just receive.

And when that space is you?

Baby... he will never forget it.

Sensuality is a sacred art.

It's not a performance. It's not a mask. It's not for show.

It's a way of being, a way of moving, feeling, tasting, receiving, expressing.

It's in your fingertips. Your breath. Your confidence. Your softness.

When you're connected to your sensuality:

- You make deeper emotional connections

- You attract passion instead of pressure

- You become unforgettable, not because of what you do, but how you are

You don't have to be "sexy."

You just have to be present.

The feminine glow comes from the inside out, and baby, when you let it flow?

Everything aligns.

CRYSTAL CARMEN REAL TALK

- Sensuality is about presence, not performance

- You don't need to be loud to be memorable

- Pleasure, passion, and softness are feminine power sources

- The more connected you are to your body, the more radiant you become

- Your sensuality is yours. You don't owe it to anyone

JOURNAL PROMPTS

What makes me feel deeply present and alive in my body?

When was the last time I truly enjoyed pleasure, without guilt?

What parts of my sensuality have I been hiding, and why?

How do I want to feel when I walk into a room?

How can I invite more sensual rituals into my daily life?

Stop Giving Wife Benefits Without a Ring

Why Courtship Still Matters and How to Attract a Marriage-Minded Man

I need you to hear me on this one , loud and clear.

If you're out here cooking, cleaning, giving him all your time, letting him move in, sleeping with him on demand, and carrying his burdens like you're already his wife... but there's no ring on your finger? You are playing yourself.

I don't say that to be harsh. I say it because too many women confuse "dating" with "auditioning for the role of unpaid wife." And the truth is, giving wife benefits to a man who hasn't committed doesn't make him step up. It makes him comfortable.

The Difference Between Girlfriend Energy and Wife Energy

Let's break this down.

Girlfriend energy is:

- Fun.

- Playful.

- Mysterious.

- Selective with access.

Wife energy is:

- Nurturing.

- Sacrificial.

- Supportive to the point of exhaustion.

- Giving without boundaries.

Now don't get me wrong , being nurturing and supportive are beautiful qualities. But timing matters. Those qualities belong in the safety of commitment, not in the uncertainty of dating.

When you hand them out too soon, you train a man to believe he can have all of you with none of the responsibility. And why would he propose when he's already reaping the benefits?

Why Courtship Still Matters

There's this lie floating around that "courtship is old-fashioned." That in today's world, we should just "go with the flow" and let things develop naturally.

But here's the thing: women who "go with the flow" usually end up in situationships.

Courtship is not outdated, it's the filter that separates men who are serious from men who are just passing time.

A man who is courting you is intentional. He's showing effort. He's investing time, energy, and consistency to prove that he wants to build something real.

A man who is not courting you? He's just hanging out.

And hanging out doesn't lead to a ring.

The Psychology Behind Why Men Value What They Earn

Men are hunters by design. They value what they pursue. They cherish what they've had to work for.

When you hand everything over without requiring pursuit, you rob him of the very process that builds value in his eyes.

Think about it. If someone gave you a designer bag for free, you might appreciate it, but not the same way you would if you had saved up, planned for it, and invested in it yourself.

It's the same with men. When they have to pursue, invest, and prove themselves, they value the relationship differently. They see you as a prize, not a convenience.

Why Women Settle Into Situationships

Here's the truth a lot of women don't want to admit: settling into wife-without-the-ring roles comes from fear.

Fear of being alone.

Fear of "losing" him if you don't give enough.

Fear that if you don't overdeliver, he'll find someone else who will.

But that fear is what keeps you stuck in half-relationships with men who were never going to marry you in the first place.

And let me tell you something that might sting: if a man walks away because you have standards, he was never yours to begin with.

The Soft Power of Standards

Here's what I know for sure, a woman with standards is irresistible to the right man and intolerable to the wrong one.

The wrong man will call you "difficult," "high maintenance," or "too much." The right man will call you "the one."

Standards aren't rules to control him. They're boundaries to protect you.

And when you embody them unapologetically, you attract men who are already marriage-minded. Why? Because they're looking for a woman who requires investment, not convenience.

How to Tell If He's Marriage-Minded

So, how do you spot a man who's serious?

Pay attention to his consistency. Courtship isn't about grand gestures once in a while. It's about steady, reliable pursuit.

Ask yourself:

- Does he plan dates or does he just "chill" at your place?

- Does he ask about your dreams or only about your body?

- Does he introduce you to his inner circle, or are you his secret?

- Does he invest in your growth, or does he just take from your energy?

If a man isn't making space for you in his real life, he's not building a future with you. He's just filling time.

My Wake-Up Call

There was a season in my life where I was doing everything for a man who hadn't even given me clarity on what we were. I was cooking, cleaning, and showing up like a full-time wife while he was still calling me "his girl."

And the worst part? I thought the harder I worked at being "wifey material," the closer I'd get to being chosen.

Wrong.

All I did was make myself convenient. And convenience doesn't inspire commitment.

When I finally pulled back, I realized something powerful: the right man doesn't need a full audition. He already knows what he wants.

The Reframe: From Wife Auditions to Queen Standards

Instead of performing, start filtering.

Instead of proving yourself, start observing.

Instead of giving it all away, start requiring consistency.

Your job isn't to convince a man you're worthy of marriage. Your job is to stand in your worth so that the right man recognizes it.

What Happens When You Stop Overgiving

Here's the beauty of pulling back from overgiving:

1. **Your value rises.** Men start to see you as a prize, not a free service.

2. **Your peace increases.** You stop stressing about doing the most to "keep" him.

3. **Your options expand.** You attract men who are serious because your standards filter out the rest.

And most importantly , you preserve your heart for the man who actually deserves it.

Crystal Carmen Real Talk

- Giving wife benefits without a ring doesn't make him commit. It makes him comfortable.

- Courtship is not outdated, it's the standard. Effort reveals intention.

- Men value what they pursue. What comes too easy rarely gets cherished.

- Fear makes women overgive. Standards make women irresistible to the right man.

- If he's not building with you, he's just passing time.

Journal Prompts
In what ways have I given "wife benefits" to a man who had not committed to me? How did that make me feel in the long run?

How do I personally define the difference between "girlfriend energy" and "wife energy"? Where am I currently blurring the lines?

What fears do I have about holding my standards? (Fear of being alone, fear of losing him, fear of being "too much"?) How have those fears shaped my past choices?

What does *being courted* look like to me? Write down 3 specific actions a man could take that would make me feel pursued and valued.

Think about the men I've dated. Who was "hanging out" versus who was "courting"? What signs did I miss in real time?

How do I usually respond when a man calls me "high maintenance" or "too much"? How do I want to respond moving forward?

Am I observing a man's consistency, or am I auditioning for his approval? What would it look like if I stopped performing and started filtering?

Where in my life can I practice pulling back from overgiving, not just in dating, but in friendships, family, or work?

What are my non-negotiable standards for partnership? (List at least 5.)

If I embodied those standards fully and unapologetically, what type of man would I attract?

MAIN CHARACTER ENERGY

The Right Man Claps the Loudest

Let me tell you something, the day you stop living like a sidekick and start living like the main character, everything changes.

Main character energy isn't about being loud, flashy, or proving yourself. It's that quiet, undeniable presence that says, "I'm her, whether you like it or not."

And let me warn you, the moment you step into it, somebody close to you is going to get real uncomfortable.

When Your Shine Makes People Squint

Not everyone claps when you win. Some folks choke on their own envy. Some will start acting brand-new. And some? They'll try to throw little obstacles in your path just to make sure you don't get too far ahead.

I had to learn the hard way that love doesn't always clap for you. Sometimes, it competes with you. Sometimes, it quietly roots against you. And sometimes, it disguises itself as support but shows up as sabotage.

Crystal's Confession

When my business started hitting real traction, I thought my relationships would naturally rise with me. I was getting orders, creating, building, finally seeing the fruits of my labor. You'd think that would mean more support, more joy, more connection.

But instead, it was the opposite.

It felt like the more I grew, the more resistance I faced. The last thing I expected was for love to feel like an anchor instead of a sail.

And then it hit me , this wasn't love. This was sabotage dressed as dependence.

That's when I realized I wasn't being treated like a partner. I was being treated like a threat.

Stop Shrinking to Make Them Comfortable

Here's the part that stings: too many of us try to fix it by shrinking. We tone down our wins. We hide our joy. We keep our dreams in our journals instead of saying them out loud. All because we don't want to make him feel "less than."

But sis, every time you shrink, you kill a little piece of yourself. And for what? For a man who can't clap when you shine? For a relationship that only works if you play small?

No. Absolutely not.

Real Men Don't Shrink. They Rise.

A high-vibrational man doesn't see your success as competition. He sees it as inspiration. He doesn't get jealous, he gets motivated. He doesn't sabotage, he strategizes with you.

If he shrinks when you shine, he's not your partner. He's your distraction.

And you can't afford distractions when you're the main character.

Crystal Carmen Real Talk: Main Character Energy

- Main character energy doesn't make the right man insecure. It makes him proud to stand next to you. And if your shine exposes his shadows, let him deal with his own darkness. Don't dim for anybody.

- A man who feels threatened by your light will never be able to protect it. Don't confuse sabotage for support.

- Your power isn't in competing with him or shrinking for him it's in choosing a partner who claps the loudest when you win.

- Real love feels like alignment, not resistance. The right man doesn't want to mute you; he wants to harmonize with you.

Journal Prompts

When was the last time you dimmed your light so someone else could feel comfortable?

How do you know the difference between love and sabotage in your own life?

What would change in your world if you showed up fully as the main character without apology?

What's one area of your life where you've been playing small, and what would "main character you" do differently?

Etiquette & Grace

The Presence of Elegance

Elegance walks into the room before you do. I can't count how many times I've seen gorgeous women who don't carry themselves in a way that says value and grace.

Grace is where most women stumble. Grace doesn't mean acting like someone's grandmother, nor does it mean being passive. It means moving with consideration, poise, and awareness of how your presence affects the room—and the man you're with.

When people are in close proximity to me for more than a few moments, I notice this shift. Some shrink into themselves, unsure of how to hold space beside my energy. Others get louder and flashier, trying to force attention back onto themselves. But when the woman is emotionally intelligent, she does something entirely different, she sits taller, adjusts, and begins to mirror the energy. That's when I always send a smile her way. Because true elegance doesn't just command respect, it invites others to rise with you.

Crystal's Confession

"I remember working with a digital marketer in Philadelphia. Before he let me into our Zoom meeting, he saw my default photo. Later he admitted it made him instantly feel awkward in his t-shirt. He actually ran to his room to change into a button-up shirt because, in his words, it just didn't feel right. That moment reminded me that true elegance sets the tone before you even speak , it makes others rise to meet your standard."

Drinks & Dining

- Limit to one or two drinks, and sip slowly. Champagne, wine, or a crafted cocktail is always more graceful than beer or shots.

- Order what you would normally order. Don't under-order to look low maintenance, and don't over-order to test his generosity. Men can tell when you're faking it.

- Always thank him for the meal and compliment either his choice of restaurant or the menu itself. Gratitude is more memorable than calculation.

Polish vs. Performance

Trying to look "high maintenance" without class always backfires. The difference is in the details.

- Clothing: Choose pieces that express your style without looking like a costume. Fit, fabric, and polish matter more than labels.

- Nails & Hands: A gel manicure is great, but quality press-ons or neatly filed and painted nails are just as elegant. What matters is care. Keep your hands soft and moisturized.

- Dressing for the Occasion: Match the energy of the environment. You don't need sequins at a 5-star restaurant, but don't show up looking like you just left the grocery store or clocked out of Sue's Gentleman's Club. Think polished, not performative.

Crystal's Confession

"Ryan never had to worry that I would show up in a way that didn't represent him well. While women should always dress for themselves, it's important to remember: when you're with a man, you also become a representation of him in every room he walks into."

Self-Care & Scent

Elegance is also about how you smell and how you care for yourself privately.

- Bathe properly. Use a soap exclusively for your girl parts and another for your body.

- Dove is not soap , it's a moisturizing bar. If you must use it, cleanse with a real soap first.

- Invest in fragrance layering. Choose rich, feminine scents like vanilla, jasmine, and orchids. A signature scent becomes part of your aura and lingers in his memory.

Elegance is Value

This is the energy you want. You want to know how to be and look everywhere you go. When you carry yourself with elegance, it makes your man, or the men pursuing you, want to hold on tighter, because you invigorate the senses and exude class.

Elegance makes a man want to get his sht together.

Let's talk money. Men invest where there is value. That includes your self-care, but also your growth. Intelligent men know where to put their time and certainly their money. When you embody grace and show that you value yourself, you signal that you are the kind of woman worthy of investment, not because you demand it, but because your presence proves it.

Rare things, like fine art, increase in value over time. The same is true for a woman who cultivates elegance. She isn't disposable, she's unforgettable. A woman who blends beauty with grace becomes the kind of presence a man never wants to lose, because she's both rare and irreplaceable.

Crystal's Confession

"I've never had to beg Ryan to invest in me, whether it was my dreams, my ideas, or my comfort. When you carry yourself as a woman of value, the right man recognizes it instantly and wants to protect, provide, and pour into you."

Crystal Carmen Real Talk

- Elegance walks in before you, posture, energy, and polish matter.

- Never test men with fake ordering habits, authenticity shows more value.

- High-maintenance without grace backfires; refinement is in the details.

- Self-care and scent are non-negotiables for a magnetic presence.

- Elegance signals value , and intelligent men invest in value.

Journal Prompts

Where in my life am I shrinking instead of sitting taller?

What's one dining habit I need to adjust to feel more graceful?

Do my nails, hair, and clothing reflect polish or performance?

What is my signature scent , and what does it say about me?

How can I embody value in a way that invites men to invest in me?

You Are Not His Mother

hy Suggestions Work Better Than Directives

Let me keep it real with you. One of the quickest ways to kill the romance in your relationship is to start treating your man like he's your child. In the words of K Michelle, "You can't rise a man, he's already grown, what you gonna do?"

Now, I know you're probably shaking your head right now thinking, "Not me, Crystal. I don't baby men." But slow down and be honest with yourself. How many times have you caught yourself saying things like:

- "Don't forget to take out the trash."

- "You need to call your mom back."

- "Did you pay that bill yet?"

- "Why don't you wear this instead of that?"

Sound familiar? Yeah, that's what I thought.

See, we slip into this pattern without even realizing it. We're capable. We're organized. We're used to handling things. And so, in a relationship, instead of letting him figure it out, we take control. But here's the harsh truth: men don't fall in love with women who mother them. They fall in love with women who inspire them.

The Difference Between Mothering and Inspiring

Children need directions. "Do your homework. Brush your teeth. Don't touch that." They depend on structure and instruction because they don't yet know how to lead themselves.

But a grown man? He doesn't need another parent. He needs a partner.

When you treat your man like a son, you unconsciously send him this message:

- I don't trust you to handle it.

- I don't believe you can figure things out.

- I have to manage you so everything gets done.

And here's the problem with that: when a man feels like he's being managed, he doesn't feel respected. And when he doesn't feel respected, attraction slowly drains out of him.

Instead of showing up as your lover, he starts showing up as your rebellious teenager or your shut-down roommate. Neither of those dynamics are sexy.

But when you shift from directive energy to suggestive energy, everything changes.

Why Suggestions Work Better

Let's break it down with examples.

Directive: "You need to take me out. We never do anything."

Suggestion: "I miss getting dressed up and being spoiled by you."

Directive: "Don't spend money on that, it's stupid."

Suggestion: "I feel more secure when we're saving for things we both want."

Directive: "Why haven't you fixed the sink yet?"

Suggestion: "It turns me on when you handle things around the house."

See the difference? The first feels like nagging. The second feels like inspiration.

Suggestions aren't weak. They're actually powerful. They don't force action, they invite it. And when you invite a man into leadership instead of demanding it, you give him the space to rise into it.

The Energy Behind It

This is more than communication tricks. It's energy.

A suggestion says:

- I trust you.

- I see you as capable.

- I believe you'll make the right move.

A directive says:

- I doubt you.

- I think I know better.

- I don't believe you'll step up unless I push you.

And here's the kicker , when you believe in him, he's more likely to rise to the occasion. When you doubt him, he'll subconsciously fulfill that expectation too.

So really, your words aren't just communication. They're prophecy.

How Mothering Turns Into Sabotage

When you constantly give orders, you train your man into what I call "slave mentality." He doesn't take initiative because he knows you'll remind him. He doesn't surprise you because he knows you'll plan it. He doesn't rise into leadership because you've already claimed it.

And then you sit there frustrated, wondering, "Why won't he step up? Why doesn't he ever take charge?"

But the truth is , he's been trained not to.

Over time, this dynamic breeds resentment. He feels smothered. You feel unsupported. Intimacy dries up. And before you know it, you're in a power struggle instead of a love story.

The 50/50 Myth and How It Feeds Mothering

Let's talk about this whole "equal partnership" trend for a second.

A lot of women today are chasing 50/50 relationships. 50/50 bills. 50/50 responsibilities. 50/50 everything. It sounds fair on paper, but in reality, it kills polarity.

Because polarity , the natural attraction between masculine and feminine , isn't about sameness. It's about difference. It's about complementing, not competing.

When you split life down the middle like roommates, guess what happens? You stop being lovers and start being business partners with benefits.

And here's the trap: when you're carrying half the load, you often end up carrying more. Because when something slips, who usually picks it up? You. That extra weight pushes you deeper into masculine energy, directing, managing, controlling, while he leans back.

And once you're in that space, you can't help but start treating him like a child. Not because you want to, but because you feel you have no choice.

That's how the cycle starts.

Why This Shows Up for High-Achieving Women

Let's get even more real. If you're a woman who's used to leading in your career, running businesses, or just being the one everybody counts on, this dynamic hits you harder.

Because leadership is natural for you. You're used to calling the shots. You're used to handling things. And so when you come home, you don't even realize you're bringing that same energy into your relationship.

But men don't want your leadership at home. They want your inspiration. They want to feel your trust, your softness, your belief in them.

If you can run empires during the day but melt into your feminine at night, you've unlocked the code to both success and love.

My Wake-Up Call

For me, the realization didn't come overnight.

I thought I was helping. I thought by reminding, managing, and directing, I was supporting the relationship. But over time, I noticed something, the more I "helped," the less supported I felt.

The more I managed, the less I was cherished.

And one day it hit me like a ton of bricks: I hadn't been a partner. I had been a mother.

That's when I made a decision. I don't want to be a man's mother. I want to be his muse. His partner. His biggest inspiration.

That meant dropping control, stepping into suggestion, and trusting that the right man doesn't shrink when I soften. He rises.

The Feminine Power Move

So how do you shift out of mother mode?

Catch Yourself in Directive Mode

Every time you start to say, "Do this, don't do that," pause. Ask yourself: Am I inspiring or am I instructing?

Reframe It

Turn the directive into a feeling-based suggestion. "I love when you take the lead on this. It makes me feel cared for.

Step Back

Yes, things may not happen on your timeline or in your exact way. But if you want polarity, you have to give space. You can't demand leadership and expect romance to thrive.

Trust His Masculine

The more you trust him, the more he'll step up. The less you trust, the less he'll try. Energy creates results.

Crystal Carmen Real Talk

- Men don't fall in love with mothers. They fall in love with muses.

- Directives sound like nagging. Suggestions sound like inspiration.

- Control suffocates polarity. Trust creates it.

- Splitting life down the middle doesn't feel like partnership , it feels like pressure.

- If you're always managing, you'll eventually resent him. If you inspire, he'll rise.

- Your feminine power isn't in telling him what to do. It's in making him want to do it.

Journal Prompts

Where have I slipped into "mother mode" in my past or current relationships?

How do I feel when I'm constantly giving directions instead of inspiring suggestions?

What would shift if I trusted men to figure things out instead of managing them?

How can I communicate my desires through feelings and inspiration instead of control?

What does being a partner , not a parent , look like for me in love?

THE COSTS OF WAITING

Why Sunken Costs Keep You Stuck in Love

Some women will hold on until their fingers bleed. They'll point to the years served, the kids born, the bills split and say, "I can't leave now , I've put in too much."

Time served is not love earned.

If you've poured ten years into a man who refuses to grow, congratulations. You don't have ten years of love. You have ten years of proof he's not changing. And the longer you stay, the more expensive the exit becomes. Not just financially,but mentally, emotionally, spiritually.

Time Doesn't Transform a Man

Time doesn't transform a man. Choices do. And if his choice has been the same nonsense for five years straight, another five won't magically turn him into Prince Charming.

Stop treating men like fine wine. Most of them expire, not age well.

I've seen women bet their entire futures on the fantasy that one day he'll wake up and say, "You know what? I'm ready now." But waiting on readiness is how you waste your prime years. You don't wait on readiness. You choose readiness. And if he hasn't chosen you fully by now, the only thing growing is your resentment.

Familiarity Isn't Commitment

Here's the wake-up call: familiarity is not commitment.

Just because you've known him for years doesn't mean he's yours. Just because you share an address doesn't mean you share a vision. And just because he hasn't left doesn't mean he's staying. Some men stay until the ride gets better somewhere else.

And in the meantime? You're breaking your own commitment, the one you should've had to yourself to protect your peace, your body, and your heart.

Every time you let yourself be a placeholder, you teach him he can treat you like one. And worse? You teach your kids the same lesson.

If you don't protect yourself, you're teaching your daughters not to either.

The Legacy of Staying Too Long

Let's talk about legacy. Women forget sometimes that kids are watching. They're not just watching how you talk to them , they're watching how you let people talk to you.

Your daughter is learning whether love means respect or survival. Your son is learning whether manhood means honor or manipulation.

When you stay in something dead, you don't just risk your own heart , you risk repeating cycles through your kids.

And one day, when your daughter asks why you let him treat you like that, what are you going to say? That you stayed because of her? That you thought sacrifice equaled strength? Trust me, kids don't want to see their mom survive , they want to see her thrive.

Death by a Thousand Cuts

The costs aren't always dramatic. Sometimes it's tiny daily wounds that bleed you out slowly.

One client told me she realized she was rushing out of her own house just to avoid her man. Think about that, your home is supposed to be your safe space, your sanctuary. If you're putting on extra errands or staying late at work just so you don't have to sit next to the person you built a life with? That's not partnership. That's prison.

Sometimes the rush to leave the house is the red flag you've been ignoring.

The Business of Bad Love

If you run a business, you know sunk costs. You know what it feels like to invest money, time, and sleepless nights into something that's dead in the water. And when you're smart, you pivot or you close the doors.

But in love? Some of you will throw good years after bad ones like it's a clearance sale.

If you'd shut down a business that's bleeding you dry, why won't you shut down a relationship doing the same?

It's wild to me how some women will spend hours analyzing their profit margins, cutting expenses, or raising prices,but won't take five minutes to audit the "man expenses" draining their soul. And make no mistake, staying with the wrong man costs you more than money. It costs you joy. It costs you energy. It costs you the life you could be building with someone who actually gives a damn.

Crystal Confessions: The Long Goodbye

I had a client who stayed in a relationship way past its expiration date. Things only got worse, but she kept holding on, convincing herself that if she loved him harder, he'd change. She poured herself out like water into cracked cement, and surprise,nothing grew.

In the end, he cheated. She was devastated. But here's the twist,her next man? He gave her the world.

Do you see the lesson? All that time and energy she spent trying to resuscitate a dead relationship could have been saved for the man who was actually ready to love her. Instead, she stayed too long, lost herself, and had to rebuild from the rubble.

Client Story: Chicken Wings & Crumbs

Another client thought she was in a relationship because a man bought her chicken wings. Let me say that again,chicken wings.

This man ate chicken wings every day. Buying her wings wasn't romantic, it was routine. But she convinced herself that crumbs of effort were grand gestures of love.

And I had to tell her, "Baby, the bar is in hell. Stop confusing scraps with steak. A man who wants you doesn't leave you guessing. He doesn't leave you confused."

The Placeholder Illusion

Some women keep men around for optics, the "look everyone, I have a man" effect. But appearances don't keep you warm at night, and fake love won't cover your emotional rent.

A warm body is not the same as a warm heart.

And when the only reason you're holding on is so your Facebook status looks good, you've already lost. You're not in a relationship,you're in a performance.

The User Marriage

Some men aren't with you for love. They're with you for access.

Your credit. Your stability. Your network.

If he loves your lifestyle more than your life, you don't have a husband. You have a dependent with benefits.

And the crazy part? A lot of women will defend that dependent harder than they defend themselves. They'll brag about "holding him down" while he's using them as a ladder.

The Hobosexual

This isn't about good men who've been down on their luck. Life happens. Good people go through hard times. I have been displaced before, so no shame on that.

I'm talking about the men who hunt for housing and call it romance. The ones who know exactly which woman to target because she's lonely, generous, and desperate for attention.

He doesn't want you. He wants your lease.

Urgency isn't love. It's survival in disguise.

And let me tell you something, ain't nobody clean your house better than a Hobosexual terrified of losing his place to stay. Don't confuse polished dishes with partnership.

The Savior Fantasy

And some of y'all like that. It feels good to say you "saved" somebody. You upgraded him. You pulled a Beyoncé.

But gratitude isn't desire, and obedience isn't intimacy.

You didn't build a husband. You built a project. And projects don't cuddle you at night.

And once that project finds a new "investor"? He'll be gone, and you'll be left holding the empty shell of all the time you wasted.

The Promise Ring Trap

And while we're here, let me bust another myth. Meeting his family doesn't mean you're "the one." And a promise ring? That's not a down payment on forever. That's a pacifier.

A man who wants you doesn't hand you a promise. He gives you a plan.

Why Women Stay

So why do women do it? Why do they stay?

Because loneliness feels unbearable. Because society tells us that being chosen, even by the wrong man, is better than being single. Because the idea of starting over feels scarier than staying stuck.

But here's the truth: loneliness inside a relationship is worse than loneliness outside of one. At least when you're single, your solitude is your own. When you're partnered but unseen? That's a prison.

Better Alone, Always

I'm not on the whole "I don't need a man" movement, obviously. I love being married now. I love being cherished. But let me tell you something: I would rather be single forever than sit in another relationship where I'm invisible.

Because the right man doesn't make you shrink. He doesn't make you guess. He doesn't leave you sitting at a dinner table wondering if anyone sees you.

The right man makes it undeniable that you are loved, chosen, and celebrated.

Crystal Carmen Real Talk

- Time served is not love earned.

- Familiarity is not commitment.

- If you wouldn't fund a failing business, don't fund a failing relationship.

- A warm body is not the same as a warm heart.

- If he loves your lifestyle more than your life, he's a dependent, not a partner.

- Urgency isn't love.

- Gratitude isn't desire.

- Projects don't cuddle you at night.

- Your kids don't need to see you survive. They need to see you thrive.

Journal Prompts

Have I ever stayed with someone just because of how long I'd been with them? What did it cost me?

Where am I mistaking history for destiny?

Do I cling to relationships for appearances instead of real intimacy?

Where in my relationship am I mistaking chores, gratitude, or survival for actual partnership?

If I treated love like the most important business decision of my life, would I keep investing, or cut my losses?

Which one of my homegirls am I secretly hating because I wish my relationship looked like hers, and what would it take for me to build my own version instead of resenting hers?

What am I teaching my children about love by the way I accept or reject treatment?

THE 4 P's—PART 1

P rotect, Provide, Preserve, Proclaim

The First P: Protection

Protection isn't just about locking doors or walking you to your car at night. It's about creating a sanctuary, a place where your body, mind, and heart are safe. A man who provides true protection doesn't just keep harm away; he creates conditions where you can finally exhale.

Protection is also about safety of expression. If you can't share your opinions, your needs, or your truth without fear of blowback, then you are not protected, you are policed.

Emotional & Mental Protection

A protective man understands that honesty isn't always comfortable, but it's necessary. He gives you space to say, "That hurt me," or "I don't agree," without punishing you for it. You should never feel like you have to water yourself down, sugarcoat your truth, or stay silent just to keep the peace.

A man who protects you listens, even when your words sting.

He doesn't weaponize your honesty against you later.

He creates an atmosphere where you feel safe saying what's on your heart, knowing your voice won't break the relationship.

Because here's the truth: if you can't be honest, you aren't safe.

Honoring Your Word

Protection is also about honoring your word. If you commit to me, then that commitment should extend to protecting my dignity, my health, and my peace of mind.

That means:

You don't put me in situations where I look foolish in front of other women, my family, or the world.

You don't run around behind my back and expose me to infections or diseases.

You don't risk breaking my heart with a love child or a "secret relationship."

You don't create conditions where I'm forced to share you, my time, or my dignity.

Protection isn't just about what happens in the streets , it's also about what happens in the bedroom, the doctor's office, the family dinner table, and in the way you carry my name in the world. Betrayal isn't only cheating; betrayal is breaking protection.

And protection can also show up in practical ways , like making sure we have health insurance, securing a safe home, and planning for the future. True protection thinks ahead: "How can I keep her covered even in ways she hasn't thought of yet?"

Red Flags of Missing Protection

You rehearse conversations in your head because you're afraid of how he'll react.

You avoid bringing things up because you know he'll blow up, shut down, or guilt-trip you.

His words and actions don't line up, leaving you constantly checking behind him.

Your truth is punished instead of received.

You get blindsided by things he could have been honest about from the start.

You feel more anxious with him than without him.

Crystal's Confession

I used to pride myself on being a strong woman who "didn't need" protection. But what I really meant was I had never experienced a relationship where it was safe to be honest. I'd test the waters with little truths, only to have them thrown back in my face later during an argument.

I also know what it feels like to be blindsided , to think I was protected, only to discover I wasn't. The betrayal wasn't just the act itself, it was the humiliation of looking foolish, the heartbreak of realizing I wasn't being covered, and the exhaustion of constantly having to protect myself from the very person who claimed to love me.

It wasn't until Ryan that I realized what true protection feels like. It's when you can say the hardest thing and still feel loved afterward. It's when you never have to wonder if someone else knows something about your relationship that you don't. It's when a man's word is so solid that your peace isn't up for negotiation. That's protection.

Crystal Carmen Real Talk:

Protection isn't only about shielding you from the outside world , it's about protecting your right to show up fully inside the relationship. It's guarding your body, your dignity, your health, and your truth. If you can't be honest, you'll never feel safe. And if you don't feel safe, your femininity will always stay guarded.

Journal Prompts

Do I feel safe expressing my needs and opinions with the men I date?

Have I ever silenced myself to avoid conflict in a relationship?

What would it look like for me to feel fully protected emotionally and mentally?

Have I ever been blindsided or humiliated in a relationship? What did that teach me about my standards now?

How will I recognize the difference between a man who tolerates my truth and a man who protects my truth?

What boundaries can I set early to ensure my health, peace, and dignity are protected?

The Second P: Provision

When people hear the word provision, most immediately think of money. And yes, financial stability is part of it, but true provision is much bigger than a paycheck. Provision is about resourcefulness, consistency, foresight, and the ability to meet needs in a way that creates security.

A man who provides isn't just handing you things, he's creating an atmosphere where you can rest, flourish, and build without constantly worrying if the basics of life will collapse underneath you. Provision is peace of mind in action.

The First Form of Provision: Dating

Here's something most people overlook: a date is actually the first form of provision. Before a man knows anything else about you, inviting you out is essentially him saying, "Allow me to provide an experience. Let me feed you, entertain you, and show you what being with me feels like."

That meal, that glass of wine, that concert ticket, that moment where he invests his resources and time into your presence, that's provision at the entry level. It shows whether he understands that part of masculine leadership is giving.

Provision Beyond the Surface

Provision deepens as the relationship deepens. It moves past dinners and flowers into stability and foresight. A truly providing man thinks: "What does she need to feel safe, covered, and cared for?"

That includes:

Financial Stability: Not just enough for today, but enough for tomorrow. He can sustain a household, not just survive in one.

Medical Coverage: A man who thinks long-term makes sure health insurance is in place. Why? Because provision isn't only about today , it's about making sure you're covered in an emergency, that bills don't destroy your peace, and that your wellbeing is prioritized.

Resourcefulness: If something breaks, he doesn't just stare at it , he fixes it, finds the right person to handle it, or makes a plan. He doesn't leave you stranded in chaos.

Consistency: You're not left wondering if he'll follow through. He says he'll handle it , and it's handled. No babysitting, no hovering, no waiting for disappointment.

Generosity: Provision is him thinking ahead: gas in your car, food in the house, your favorite drink already waiting because he paid attention. It's him anticipating needs, not just responding when you cry out for help.

Provision is about security , not just in the moment, but long-term.

The 50/50 Debate

Let's address the elephant in the room: 50/50.

Some couples thrive splitting everything evenly, and I won't knock that. But over time, I've learned it doesn't work for me. And before anyone assumes, "Oh, she just wants somebody to pay for everything," let me be clear: I've been on both sides of the coin. I've carried the whole load. I've split it down the middle. I've even been the bread-winner. So this isn't about entitlement , it's about alignment.

Here's my truth: it doesn't feel good to roll over in the morning and have a man breathing down my neck about half the bills. I don't want a roommate. I want a partner. And for me, true provision means knowing the essentials are covered without having to compete, negotiate, or fight to feel safe in my own home.

When provision is secure, I can relax. I can give more of my softness, my creativity, my nurturing, my vision. I'm not weighed down by the masculine role of carrying everything. Provision frees me to be who I really am.

Crystal's Confession The Top Shelf Pretender

I remember a former girlfriend of mine who thought my "I don't do 50/50" ideology was unfair and unrealistic. She'd say things like, "I don't need to worry if a man has money, because I do."

Fast forward, she's dating this new guy, and for a short while I was actually her roommate. The first time I met him, something was already off. This was his very first visit, yet he had his shoes kicked off and his feet up on her chaise lounge like he owned the place. That's not second-date behavior , that's entitlement showing up early.

Later, we went downstairs to her basement bar. I offered them both a drink. He declined at first, then suddenly changed his mind and said, "You know what, I'll take a drink... give me whisky, I said what kind, he couldnt name one, then he say okay top shelpd, top shelf."

Now, who even says that? Not "I'll take a whiskey," not "What do you recommend?" , but "Give me something top shelf." So I poured him exactly what he asked for, a double shot of top-shelf whiskey. He immediately choked on it.

That moment told me everything I needed to know. His mannerisms, his choice of words, even the fact that he didn't know a single brand but still asked for "top shelf" , it screamed inexperience, posturing, and the need to perform provision instead of actually embodying it.

Provision isn't about pretending. It's not about flexing. It's not about being flashy on dates and then asking a woman to split the light bill later. True provision is steady, quiet confidence. It doesn't need to announce itself as "top shelf" , because it is.

Crystal's Confession II: The Applebee's Math

Flash forward again: she and this same man go out on a date to Applebee's. The bill comes, and he only has $20 to put toward it. She ends up paying the rest and is so flabbergasted she doesn't talk to him the entire ride home. Later she calls me, venting.

And I asked her a serious question: "What did you expect?"

Then I broke it down for her. "How many times do you expect to be taken out by the man you're with?"

She answered, "Two to three times a week."

So let's do the math:

Two to three times a week at Applebee's? That's $80 a date.

At the places she and I normally went? That's $100+ a meal.

Which means $300 a week, $1,200 every two weeks, and about $2,400 a month , just on dining.

Now add in his car note, his apartment, his bills, his desires, and his own life expenses. That means the man she expected to wine and dine her three times a week would need to see $2,400 per month as discretionary income without jeopardizing his well-being.

In other words: you need a man who makes enough for that expectation to be realistic.

This same man had also asked her to put $1,000 down for their vacation because he couldn't cover the deposit himself , though he promised he'd "handle the tickets" later. He even wanted her to cover the drink package. At that point, she finally admitted that it was unreasonable to expect a man who wasn't earning enough to provide the lifestyle she envisioned.

The Hidden Truth About Provision

And here's where so many women trip up: none of this would have been a problem if she was truly okay covering the difference on a regular basis. Some women are, and that's fine. But she wasn't.

She was so busy verbally disagreeing with my ideology that she didn't see her subconscious expectations lining up with it. On the surface she said, "I don't need a man's money because I have my own." But deep down, she still wanted the dinners, the vacations, the experiences , and she wanted him to provide them.

This is where so many well-to-do women get frustrated. They say they don't care if he has money because they do. But then months or years into the relationship, they're resentful because he's not providing the life they secretly expect. They cover the gaps, start nagging, and grow bitter , all while the man feels inadequate and confused.

That's not fair to either person. Because if you want more than what he's capable of, you'll always feel unfulfilled. And if he's giving his all but it's never enough, he'll always feel like a failure.

We're not talking about men on the brink of their potential , the ones building, moving, and working toward provision in a consistent, calculable way. Those men are worth standing beside. But if a man isn't willing or able to move in that direction, then being with him with unexpressed expectation is not just cruel it's just wasting your time and his.

Provision Is Not Just Six Figures

And let me say this clearly: being a provider does not mean a man has to earn six figures.

If I had a dollar for every man podcaster repeating the tired line that women only want the "six-foot, six-figure guy," I'd be a billionaire. Provision is not tied to a number.

I've lived in public housing before, so I say this with no shame: if a woman meets a man who helps her move out of public housing into stability, provides a safe home, and builds from there, that man is a provider. Even if he doesn't hit six figures.

Provision is about sustaining the environment, protecting peace of mind, and providing safety, security, and shelter.

Now, expectations scale with lifestyle. If your dream is two or three Birkins a year, let's do the math: those bags are $10,000 to $50,000+ each. That means you're not looking for a six-figure man, you're looking for someone who earns significantly more. Because the math has to math.

So stop tying provision to a dollar figure. Tie it to consistency, stability, and whether or not he can sustain the kind of life you actually want to live.

CrystaL Carmen Real Talk

Provision isn't about greed or gold-digging. It's about alignment. A man who provides doesn't just give material things, he gives peace of mind. If you secretly want more than a man can provide, you'll end up resentful, and he'll end up feeling like he's never enough. But when provision is aligned, when his ability matches your desires, both of you can flourish.

Journal Prompts

Do I feel provided for, financially, emotionally, and practically, in my relationships?

What does provision look like for me?

Am I willing to do the financial heavy lifting, and do so contenly and without resentment?

How do I view provision: as money, as peace of mind, or as both?

Have I ever carried the full weight of provision in a partnership? How did that affect me?

How do I want a man's provision to show up in both small ways (dates, daily needs) and big ways (insurance, stability, long-term planning)?

What boundaries can I set to avoid stepping into the role of over-provider?

What does feeling carefree in my relationship look like for me, and what kind of provision makes that possible?

Are my expectations of provision aligned with the kind of man I'm dating , or are they quietly unrealistic?

THE 4 P's PART 2

P rotect, Provide, Preserve, Proclaim

The Third P: Preservation

Provision is about providing, but preservation is about protecting what's already there, your peace, your health, your beauty, your energy, your essence.

A man who values preservation doesn't just want you to shine for the world , he actively helps you stay shining. He recognizes that your femininity is delicate yet powerful, and instead of draining it, he safeguards it.

Preservation is also about him preserving what he has built , his integrity, his assets, his legacy , so that what you're creating together is not jeopardized.

What Preservation Looks Like

Preserving Peace: He doesn't bring chaos into your life. He manages his own emotions, minimizes unnecessary drama, and resolves conflict instead of creating it.

Preserving Energy: He doesn't drain you with constant problems, poor planning, or emotional instability. Instead, he helps lighten your load so you have more energy for the things you love.

Preserving Integrity: He avoids situations that could compromise your goals, embarrass the relationship, or jeopardize what you're building together. He knows one reckless decision could undo years of progress, and he values you both too much to risk it.

Preserving Legacy: He thinks ahead. He invests, he gets life insurance, he plans. He ensures that if, God forbid, something happens, you'll be okay. You won't lose the house, the stability, or the life you've built together. Preservation means he doesn't just live for today; he protects tomorrow.

Preserving Dignity: He makes choices that honor your name, your reputation, and your place in his life.

Preservation is about recognizing that once something valuable is created, it must be cared for, not neglected, squandered, or destroyed.

Red Flags of Missing Preservation

He takes unnecessary risks that could cost him (and you) everything.

He makes impulsive financial decisions that jeopardize stability.

He acts like life is invincible, avoiding conversations about insurance, planning, or protection.

He undermines your shared goals with selfish or reckless behavior.

You notice your spark, glow, or peace fading because you're carrying what he refuses to preserve.

Crystal's Confession

I've been in relationships where I felt like everything we were building together was always one bad decision away from collapsing. Whether it was financial recklessness, poor planning, or lack of foresight, I realized that without preservation, all the provision in the world eventually gets wasted.

With my marriage now, I learned what true preservation looks like. It's not just about how he treats me day to day, it's how he protects what we're building. He invests. He plans. He makes sure that if something ever happened, I would be okay. That kind of foresight doesn't just protect the present, it protects the future. That's preservation.

Crystal Carmen Real Talk

Provision provides. Preservation sustains. A man who truly loves you will not just help you grow, he will help you maintain. Preservation is about guarding peace, health, beauty, and dignity, and protecting the life you're building together through integrity, responsibility, and foresight. If being with him feels like living on the edge of collapse, he isn't preserving you, he's gambling with you.

Journal Prompts

Do I feel like the men I date or commit to preserve my peace and energy, or do they deplete it?

Have I ever been with someone who put what we were building at risk through recklessness? How did that affect me?

What does financial and legacy preservation look like to me (insurance, investments, stability, etc.)?

How can I better communicate that preservation of our future is just as important to me as provision today?

What boundaries can I set to ensure the life I build with someone is preserved, not jeopardized?

The Fourth P: Proclamation

The final "P" is proclamation , the way a man claims you, honors you, and makes your place in his life clear.

Proclamation is about visibility and certainty. It's not just about saying, "I love you," in private. It's about making sure you never have to wonder where you stand, because his words and actions consistently affirm you in public and in private.

What Proclamation Looks Like

Public Acknowledgment: He introduces you proudly as his partner. There's no hiding, no confusion, no "situationship."

Private Consistency: He affirms you in daily ways , through his affection, words, and actions , so you feel claimed even when no one's watching.

Alignment With You: He lives in a way that says, "I choose her." Not only through social media or appearances, but in decisions that keep you at the center of his life.

Clarity in Relationship Status: There's no gray area. You don't have to guess whether you're the girlfriend, the fiancée, the wife, he makes sure you know, and so does everyone else.

Why Proclamation Matters

A woman in love shouldn't live in limbo. If you constantly wonder where you stand, you'll never relax into your feminine energy. Proclamation matters because it eliminates doubt. It says: "You are my person, and I am proud of it."

It's not just about posting you on social media , though that's one expression. It's about the consistent reassurance that you are chosen, you are secure, and you are not hidden.

Red Flags of Missing Proclamation

He avoids labels or refuses to "define the relationship."

You feel hidden , he never posts you, brings you around family, or makes introductions.

You hear excuses like, "I don't like PDA," or, "I'm private," but somehow that "privacy" only benefits him.

His words about you don't match his actions with you.

You feel like you're constantly proving you belong instead of knowing you do.

When Proclamation is Missing

Consider the example of a woman who has been with her partner for four years. He earns six figures and regularly spends on travel, sports, and costly hobbies. Yet his excuse for not proposing has always been that he is "waiting until he can afford the proper ring."

This is not about money , she has been clear that she does not need an expensive ring or wedding. This is about priorities. Despite financial means, he has not even taken the basic step of finding out what kind of ring she would like. To the outside world, they appear rarely together, to the point that people in their own community cannot identify them as a couple.

At home, when she is unwell, he continues going out and doing what he enjoys, leaving her to manage alone. On paper, he covers most of the rent. But without proclamation, protection, or preservation, provision becomes little more than bill-paying.

This is what the absence of proclamation looks like: a woman left unclaimed, unacknowledged, and unsupported while the man continues to live freely.

The Open Door of Neglect

When proclamation is missing, it leaves blanks , and human beings are wired to fill blanks. In relationships, if a man consistently fails to provide clarity, attention, or security, others will step in. Family, friends, even strangers will naturally occupy the spaces he leaves open.

That's exactly what happens in relationships where a woman is un-proclaimed. She begins leaning on others for the protection, provision, or preservation her partner withholds. And if this continues long enough, she becomes vulnerable to the attention of someone else , even someone only pretending to "save" her.

This isn't always about her seeking it out. It's about him leaving her uncovered. Proclamation isn't just about pride or titles; it's a safeguard. When a woman is clearly, visibly, and consistently proclaimed, there is no room for confusion and far less room for outsiders to slide into the space he neglected.

Crystal's Confession

I've been in relationships where I had to beg for clarity. Where I was kept in the shadows, downplayed, or treated like an option. That kind of silence feels like rejection, even when you're technically "together."

The difference with Ryan is that I've never had to fight for proclamation. He makes it clear where I stand , not just to me, but to everyone else. When he introduces me, it's with pride. When life gets busy, I still feel chosen. That kind of consistent proclamation doesn't just affirm me; it makes our relationship stronger, because there's no room for doubt to creep in.

Crystal Carmen Real Talk

Proclamation is about clarity and honor. It's how a man communicates, "You are mine, and I am proud of that fact." A man who proclaims you takes away confusion, silences insecurity, and makes you feel secure in both private and public spaces. Without proclamation, you're left guessing. With proclamation, you're left glowing.

Proclamation in Commitment

Proclamation doesn't stop at introductions or daily reassurances. If you are clear that you want marriage, then proclamation means he gives you the ring. Period.

Because let's be real: if a man knows he wants to marry you, he doesn't waste years "acting married" without ever sealing it with commitment. A ring is not just jewelry , it's a declaration. It's him proclaiming to the world, "This is my wife. I choose her, permanently, and I'm building my life with her."

Without that level of proclamation, you're left in limbo. With it, you're secured in clarity, in honor, and in future.

Red Flags of Missing Proclamation

He avoids labels or refuses to "define the relationship."

You feel hidden, he never posts you, introduces you, or makes introductions.

He downplays commitment with excuses like, "I'm just private," but that privacy only benefits him.

Years go by without clarity, engagement, or movement toward marriage , even though he knows that's what you want.

You feel like you're constantly proving your place instead of knowing you're secure in it.

The Bigger Truth

The ring itself is not everything. Provision alone is not everything. Preservation alone is not everything. Proclamation alone is not everything.

Independently, none of the Ps can sustain a relationship. A man may provide financially, but without preservation she withers. He may proclaim her with a ring, but without protection she is unsafe. He may preserve his assets, but without proclaiming her, she still feels invisible.

To be truly safe, honored, secure, and protected, all four Ps must work in sync. That is when a woman can finally exhale and rest in the fullness of love.

Crystal's Confession

I've been in relationships where I was kept in the shadows , not introduced, not acknowledged, and certainly not proclaimed. It made me feel like I was begging for clarity when all I really wanted was to feel chosen.

The difference with Ryan is that I've never had to wonder. He doesn't hesitate to let the world know who I am to him. His proclamation isn't just in words , it's in actions, consistency, and the way he

honors me both publicly and privately. And yes, it's also in the ring ,
the visible sign that I am spoken for, protected, and cared for.

Crystal Carmen Real Talk

Proclamation is about clarity and honor. It's how a man communicates, "You are mine, and I am proud of that fact." The ring is the
universal proclamation. Without it, you are still waiting. With it, you
are chosen, claimed, and secured.

Journal Prompts

Do I feel publicly and privately claimed in my relationships, or
hidden?

Have I ever felt like people in my own community couldn't tell I
was in a relationship? How did that affect me?

How do I want proclamation to show up for me , introductions,
affection, consistency, a ring, or all of the above?

Have I ever felt hidden in a relationship? How did that affect my
confidence and sense of security?

What is the difference for me between being acknowledged and
being truly proclaimed?

Am I being honest about whether I want marriage, and am I aligned
with a man who wants to proclaim me in that way?

How do I want proclamation to show up for me, introductions,
transparency, consistency, a ring, or all of the above?

Am I aligned with a man who is proactive about declaring me his partner?

How will I recognize a man who proclaims me without hesitation?

If I want marriage, a I with a man who is moving toward proclamation with a ring and also showing protection, provision, and preservation?

THE TWIN FLAME MYTH

I t may be trauma bonding...or a narcissist.

Why Intensity Isn't Always Intimacy

If I had $2 for every time I heard a woman bring up "the twin flame thing," I'd be sitting on a pile of cash. And here's the pattern I've noticed: it almost always comes up when the relationship is a hot mess. There's constant conflict, back-and-forth drama, push and pull, and the woman is clinging to something that doesn't make sense.

Instead of calling it what it is,chaos,she calls it destiny.

She calls it her twin flame.

Trauma Bonding Dressed as Destiny

Let's be clear. Most of the time when women start talking about twin flames, what they're really describing is trauma bonding and codependency.

They want this person so badly, they'll create meaning out of the mess. They'll convince themselves that the arguing, the inconsistency, the highs and lows are all part of some cosmic test from God or the universe.

I've even seen it with women who don't consider themselves "spiritual." They get caught in the idea that because they like some of the same things, or had an instant connection, this must be "meant to be."

But let me tell you the truth: if your relationship feels like constant push and pull, if it's back and forth all the time, if you're being made to feel unworthy, discarded, or unstable,that's not your twin flame. That's dysfunction.

What the "Twin Flame" Definition Gets Twisted

I've read the definitions. I know the spin: a twin flame is supposed to be the person who mirrors your flaws, who highlights what you need to work on. The one who "triggers" you into growth.

Sounds deep, right?

But here's the problem: that same logic has women staying in situations where they're constantly hurt, constantly doubting themselves, constantly excusing bad behavior because they believe it's all "part of the lesson."

No. If your "twin flame" makes you question your worth, if they manipulate, abandon, or mistreat you,then they're not your destiny. They're your distraction.

The Manipulation Trap

And let's get real: men today don't even have to lie.

If you've overshared early,if you've trauma-dumped on date two, if you've given a man your whole life story before he's earned it,you've already given him the blueprint to play you. He now knows exactly what to say and do to mirror you back to yourself.

That's not a connection. That's manipulation.

And once he pulls you in, once you've convinced yourself this is your cosmic twin flame, you'll justify anything. Because you'd rather believe this is God testing you than admit you've been duped.

The Psychology of Oversharing

One of the sneakiest traps that makes women believe they've met their "twin flame" is how much they reveal, how soon.

Here's the truth: when you pour out your soul in the first few dates or late-night calls, you create a false sense of intimacy. Your brain starts releasing oxytocin (the bonding hormone) as if this person has earned your vulnerability, when really, they've just been sitting there listening.

This is how a lot of women trick themselves into thinking, "I feel so close to him, like I've known him forever."

But what's really happening is chemistry mixed with confession , not true compatibility.

And here's the dangerous part: once you hand over your entire emotional blueprint, the wrong man now knows exactly how to play you.

- You tell him about your daddy issues? Now he mirrors protectiveness or uses it to test your loyalty.

- You tell him your favorite artists or books? Suddenly, he "loves them too."

- You tell him what you've been craving in a partner? He performs it for 30 days, then disappears.

This is why oversharing too soon isn't vulnerability. It's self-sabotage.

Because you've just given him the cheat codes to your heart without requiring him to show who he really is first.

Crystal Carmen Real Talk

Listen. If someone seems "perfect" after you've poured your whole life story into their lap, chances are, they're reflecting you back at yourself, not showing you their true self.

That's not fate. That's performance.

Why It's So Hard to Walk Away

There's a saying I love: "A man convinced against his will is of the same opinion still."

That's why it's so hard to talk your girlfriend out of one of these relationships. Or even talk yourself out of it. Because deep down, you don't want to go. You don't want to be alone. You don't want to start over.

So it's easier to trick yourself into believing this is fated. That if you just wait long enough, love hard enough, change everything about yourself, he'll finally wake up and see you as "the one."

That's not love. It's delusion.

Anything that's truly for you is not running from you, not like that.

Crystal's Confession

I had a client who swore her man was her twin flame. She told me they dreamed of each other. They'd see each other in visions, in dreams, in "signs."

Do I believe two people can feel connected on a soul level? Sure.

Do I believe two people can both dream of each other simply because they're constantly on one another's minds? Absolutely.

Do I believe that means he was her soulmate who was eventually going to "wake up" and transform into a loving, faithful, committed man? Absolutely not.

And here's why: no dream, no sign, no "unexplainable pull" is going to turn a manipulative, inconsistent man into the man you deserve.

That requires his choice. His effort. His growth.

And you cannot earn love through suffering.

You cannot work, cry, or "prove yourself" into being chosen.

Why Women Confuse Chaos with Love

Part of this is biology.

Sex, hormones, and emotional highs create a powerful chemical cocktail in your brain. Oxytocin and dopamine bond you to a man, even when he's toxic. That's why the highs feel so addictive.

Part of it is culture. Movies, books, and songs romanticize dysfunction. They tell us "the best love stories are the hardest," or "if he doesn't fight for you, it's not real."

And part of it is trauma. If you grew up in a home where love meant chaos, inconsistency, or pain, your nervous system might mistake anxiety for passion.

The Real Mark of Love

Here's the truth no one wants to say out loud:

Real love isn't obsessive. It's consistent.

Real love doesn't make you feel sick. It makes you feel safe.

Real love doesn't confuse you. It clarifies everything.

The man meant for you will not require you to beg, suffer, or sacrifice your self-worth just to hold his attention.

If he's constantly running, abandoning, or discarding you, that's not fate. That's who he is.

Crystal Carmen Real Talk

- Intensity without consistency is chaos.

- If you need him to hurt you before you feel close, that's not a soulmate. That's a trauma bond.

- Twin flames don't test your sanity. They bring peace.

- You cannot love someone into changing. They have to want it.

- Anything truly meant for you doesn't leave you in pieces.

Journal Prompts

Have I ever confused chaos or intensity with true intimacy?

Do I believe love has to be hard to be real? Where did that belief come from?

What's one example from my past where I called a man "meant for me," but deep down I knew he wasn't?

What would it feel like to only accept love that makes me feel safe and steady?

Am I willing to release the fantasy of "twin flames" in order to embrace a real, healthy relationship?

Do You Even Know What Kind of Man You Want Anyway?

Because if you can't name him, you're probably just entertaining whoever shows up.

Let's get brutally honest:

You say you want a man who's high-value, emotionally intelligent, consistent, confident, faithful, fun, sexy, successful, spiritual, secure, and supportive...

But if I asked you to describe him without using generic Pinterest affirmations, could you?

Or are you just hoping the next guy isn't a total dumpster fire?

Imagine that I told you to meet me in the airport but you have never seen me before. You don't know how I dress, you don't know how tall I am and you don't know what my fave features are. Could you imagine if you had to find me in a sea of people? Where would you begin? How would you know me when you saw me? If I was standing in front of you the whole time you would never know even if you had my voice to go on.

This chapter is the mirror you didn't know you needed.

Because half the time, women end up in messy, misaligned situations not because "there are no good men," but because they've never taken the time to figure out who the hell they actually want.

Not what's cute. Not what your girls think.

Not who gives you butterflies.

But the kind of man who makes your soul feel safe while your body stays lit.

If you don't know where you're going any path will take you there.

WHY YOU KEEP PICKING THE WRONG MEN

Let's be clear, it's not always your fault.

You picked what you were taught to pick.

What you were raised around.

What your body responded to in trauma, not truth.

You learned to fall for men who were emotionally unavailable...

Because that was your normal.

You confused inconsistency with mystery.

You mistook anxiety for attraction.

You let potential dress up as personality.

And now here you are, tired, disappointed, and done with the bare minimum.

But the truth is:

You can't attract what you don't define.

You can't get what you want until you know exactly what that is, and believe you deserve it.

FANTASY VS. FUNCTIONAL LOVE

It's cute to say you want a provider.

It's even cuter to say you want a man who takes initiative, opens doors, buys flowers, plans trips, and helps build your dreams...

But can you hold a man like that?

Do you know how to:

- Let him lead without fighting for control?

- Receive love without performing for it?

- Trust someone without testing them to death?

- Speak your needs without trying to parent him?

High-value men don't want to be managed.

They want to be magnetized.

And until you know what kind of man you're trying to attract, you'll keep playing romantic roulette with men who look the part... and then flip the script.

Crystal's Confession

At one point, I thought I wanted a man who was "on his grind", up at 5 a.m., always working, always building.

You know, the "hustler with a heart."

Until I realized... I was exhausted.

I didn't need a man who was always gone, trying to prove something.

I needed a man who made space.

A man who could slow down, ask how I was doing, and rub my feet without me begging.

Once I got clear on that?

Once I understood that I didn't want the fast life, I wanted the deep life?

I stopped falling for hype men and started attracting grounded, solid, steady love.

Because the man I actually wanted... wasn't loud.

He was intentional.

STOP TREATING RED FLAGS LIKE CHALLENGES

You're not here to rehab men.

You're not the director of a personal development bootcamp.

If you know what you want, then the moment you see he isn't that, walk.

Not after 90 days.

Not after another 3 "just talks."

Immediately.

Red flags are not puzzles to decode.

They are revelations.

The right man won't confuse you.

You won't have to guess his intentions.

And he will not be intimidated by your softness or your strength.

KNOWING WHAT YOU WANT MEANS YOU DON'T GET LOST WHEN LOVE SHOWS UP

When a good man arrives, will you know how to receive him?

Or will you sabotage it because it's unfamiliar?

Will you project old fears onto new beginnings?

Will you cling to independence because you never learned how to be supported?

You say you want partnership.

But do you want it enough to be honest with yourself about:

- Your expectations

- Your communication style

- Your emotional triggers

- Your trust wounds

- Your beliefs about men, love, and intimacy?

Because clarity is queen energy.

It protects your time. It weeds out nonsense.

And it attracts men who are ready, not just interested.

YOUR LOVE LIST (THE RIGHT WAY)

Let's build the man you actually want, not the Instagram version, not the checklist your mama gave you.

Ask yourself:

- How do I want to feel when I'm with him?

- What are his natural habits, not what I'd have to beg him to learn?

- How does he handle conflict?

- How does he treat women who can't give him anything?

- What kind of peace does he protect in our home?

And while you're at it, What kind of woman does he need me to be to receive him fully?

Not a perfect one.

But one who is self-aware, aligned, and rooted in what's real.

If you don't know what kind of man you want, every man will look like an option.

And most of them aren't.

So get clear.

Get confident.

And stop mistaking chemistry for compatibility.

Because your forever love?

He's not going to be "close enough."

He's going to match the list you finally decided you were worthy of.

And if you need to write him out, pray over him, visualize him, or vibe in silence until he shows up, do it.

But don't you dare keep settling just because you didn't take the time to define your actual desire.

CRYSTAL CARMEN REAL TALK

- You can't attract what you don't define

- Fantasy men are fun, but real love needs real clarity

- Red flags are answers, not maybe signs

- A good man will not require a personality transplant, just your truth

- High-value men are not impressed by potential, they're drawn to aligned peace

JOURNAL PROMPTS

How do I want to feel in my next relationship?

What traits are non-negotiable, and what things don't
actually matter as much as I thought?

Have I been confusing intensity with intimacy?

What does a healthy love actually look like for me?

Am I the kind of woman my dream man is praying for?

THE STANDARDS GAME

Redefining What You Really Want in a Man

By now you've read the stories, done the journal prompts, and hopefully had more than one "aha" moment about how you've been dating. But here's where we bring it all together.

This last chapter isn't just about reading. It's about choosing.

Because if you don't know what you truly want, you'll keep saying yes to what you don't.

It's Okay to Want What You Want

Let me clear the air: it's okay to want a man with money. It's okay to want a man who's tall, ambitious, handsome, successful. You're human. We all have preferences.

But here's where women get tripped up: they stop at the surface.

A rich man who isn't generous will leave you feeling unappreciated.

A rich man who is reckless with his money will make you feel unstable.

A rich man who uses money to control you will leave you powerless.

So the real standard isn't "rich." It's "financially responsible." It's "generous." It's "secure enough in his success that he wants to share it with you."

See the difference?

- "Rich" is about what he has.

- "Financially responsible and generous" is about who he is.

And who he is will determine how you feel every single day you share a life with him.

Why Surface Qualities Will Never Be Enough

You can have a handsome man who is unfaithful and needs constant attention from other women to feel good about himself.

You can find a church-going man who talks about faith on Sunday but drinks his money away by Friday.

You can have a man with money who spends every waking hour chasing more, but has no compassion and no time left to actually share life with you.

Do you see the pattern? Surface-level labels don't guarantee soul-level security.

This is why your list has to go deeper than "handsome, rich, religious, ambitious." Because you can have all of that and still end up lonely in a relationship.

The question isn't just what does he have? or what does he look like? The real question is: how will I feel in this relationship with him?

Crystal's Confession

Don't think your list is unrealistic or untenable.

I never once wrote "tall" on mine, yet I ended up with a husband who's 6'3". Not because I asked for it, but because I asked for a man who made me feel safe, consistent, and strong in character. Height was just the bonus.

That's the beauty of clarity , when you set standards rooted in values, the extras often show up anyway.

Stop Chasing Labels. Start Defining Values.

Instead of asking for "rich," ask for financially responsible.

Instead of "educated," ask for a man who values intelligence.

Instead of "romantic," ask for a man who is emotionally intelligent enough to notice what makes you feel loved.

Instead of "buys me things," ask for a man who enjoys giving gifts because it brings him joy.

When you change the language of your standards, you don't just change your list , you change the type of men who show up.

The Standards Game

So here's how we're ending this book: with a game.

Below is a massive list of traits, values, and qualities. Your challenge is simple:

Circle no more than 15–20.

Yes, only 15–20.

Because if everything is important, nothing is. This game forces you to prioritize and get painfully honest with yourself. Do you want a man who makes you laugh more than one who makes six figures? Do you want consistency over charm? Do you value vision more than romance?

This list is about clarity. And clarity is the foundation of attraction.

The Standards List

☐ Loyalty

☐ Integrity

- ☐ Humor
- ☐ Consistency
- ☐ Kindness
- ☐ Emotional intelligence
- ☐ Ambition
- ☐ Patience
- ☐ Self-control
- ☐ Respect for women
- ☐ Empathy
- ☐ Ability to lead with humility
- ☐ Financial responsibility
- ☐ Family-oriented
- ☐ Spiritually grounded
- ☐ Good communicator
- ☐ Conflict resolution skills
- ☐ Generosity
- ☐ Work ethic
- ☐ Protectiveness
- ☐ Vision for the future
- ☐ Accountability
- ☐ Honesty
- ☐ Adaptability
- ☐ Confidence (not arrogance)
- ☐ Supportive of your dreams
- ☐ Discipline
- ☐ Maturity
- ☐ Gratitude
- ☐ Dependability
- ☐ Respectful of boundaries
- ☐ Passion for growth

☐ Nurturing

☐ Makes you feel safe emotionally & physically

☐ Romantic effort

☐ Ability to apologize and repair

☐ Keeps his word

☐ Protects your peace

☐ Treats service people kindly

☐ Practices gratitude

☐ Focused on legacy/future planning

☐ Values intelligence

☐ Appreciates art or creativity

☐ Good with children

☐ Healthy relationship with family

☐ Not addicted to substances

☐ Manages stress well

☐ Willing to go to therapy if needed

☐ Cares about health and wellness

☐ Keeps commitments

☐ Encourages your self-care

☐ Doesn't compete with you

☐ Celebrates your wins

☐ Stable in career or purpose

☐ Doesn't weaponize silence

☐ Listens without dismissing

☐ Makes time for you

☐ Enjoys giving gifts

☐ Shows initiative in planning

☐ Doesn't belittle your feelings

☐ Problem-solver

☐ Open to growth and learning

- ☐ Respectful in disagreements
- ☐ Protects your reputation
- ☐ Doesn't make you beg for basics
- ☐ Considers your needs before decisions
- ☐ Doesn't flirt with everyone
- ☐ Respects privacy
- ☐ Gives compliments freely
- ☐ Shares responsibilities
- ☐ Has ambition beyond bare minimum
- ☐ Cares about community
- ☐ Values legacy over ego
- ☐ Uses money wisely
- ☐ Appreciates effort you put in
- ☐ Keeps promises small and large
- ☐ Doesn't break trust casually
- ☐ Emotionally stable
- ☐ Playful and fun
- ☐ Can handle pressure without crumbling
- ☐ Doesn't run from conflict
- ☐ Motivates you to be better
- ☐ Sees you as a partner, not competition
- ☐ Enjoys intimacy, not just sex
- ☐ Has discipline in daily life
- ☐ Doesn't embarrass you publicly
- ☐ Kind to strangers
- ☐ Has backbone, not just charm
- ☐ Walks in integrity when no one is watching
- ☐ Doesn't manipulate with guilt
- ☐ Loves learning
- ☐ Isn't cheap with money or love

☐ Encourages friendships, not isolation

☐ Knows how to compromise

☐ Protects your emotional safety

☐ Doesn't play games with communication

☐ Reliable in emergencies

☐ Lives with purpose

☐ Respects your body

☐ Admits mistakes

☐ Keeps growing, doesn't stay stagnant

Crystal Carmen Real Talk:

- It's okay to want "rich" or "handsome" or "successful." But without the values behind them, those qualities will frustrate you.

- How you word your standards matters: rich attracts rich; responsible attracts steady.

- Height, muscles, and charm might be nice , but safety, consistency, and integrity will last.

- You only get 15–20 standards. If you circle them all, you're not serious about clarity.

- The right man doesn't check every box , but he checks the boxes that matter most.

Journal Prompts

What surface-level standards have I clung to in the past? Did they get me what I truly wanted?

How can I reframe those standards into deeper values (e.g., "rich" → "financially responsible and generous")?

When I think about how I want to feel in a relationship, what qualities support that feeling?

Which 15–20 standards did I circle from the list, and why those?

What will I do differently the next time I feel tempted to compromise on those standards?

How to Take Care of a Man

How to Take Care of a Man

We spend so much time talking about what men should bring to the table, protection, provision, preservation, proclamation. But love is reciprocal. Once you have a man who shows up for you, you also have a responsibility to show up for him.

Taking care of a man doesn't mean babying him or becoming his mother. It means loving him in ways that honor his masculinity while also nurturing his humanity. A healthy man flourishes when his woman knows how to give love, affection, and even sternness in balance.

Love

Love is in the details. It's not always the grand gestures, it's the little ways you pay attention.

Put the phone down when he's talking or when he finally has time to relax.

Don't immediately ask him to do something the moment he settles in after work. Give him breathing room.

If you have children, create a half-hour buffer before you or the kids rush him with asks. Let him decompress and reconnect with his family first.

If you get home later than he does, don't walk in and unload complaints in the first few minutes. Let him see his woman, enjoy your energy, and settle into your presence before you tell him about Jessica at the office.

Ask about his day and listen without rushing to give advice.

Take him out to lunch or for a coffee sometimes, let him feel pursued and appreciated too.

Say thank you when he puts in effort, instead of brushing it off.

Randomly tell him you appreciate him.

Love is expressed when you show him you notice his efforts, his energy, and his presence.

Affection

Men love gentle touches, caresses, kisses in passing, and intimacy that feels intentional. Affection is not weakness , it's connection.

Watch a movie he likes.

Surprise him with his favorite meal or snack if he loves food.

Offer foot massages and back rubs , men love being cared for physically too.

Cuddle and touch without it always having to lead to sex.

Compliment him on how he looks or smells, men notice when you notice.

Affection says: I don't just want you here, I enjoy you here.

Sternness

Sternness is boundaries wrapped in love. It's not nagging, it's accountability.

"I love you, but I won't tolerate being spoken to that way."

Hold him accountable to his word, if he says he'll handle something, you expect follow-through.

Remind him of who he is when he slips into doubt or excuses.

Sternness is how you keep the relationship strong. A man respects a woman who can check him with grace.

Gifts & Celebrations

Gifts matter. Birthdays, holidays, and milestones are opportunities to make him feel seen.

Don't just grab socks, figure out what he actually likes.

If he loves experiences, get tickets to a game, a concert, or plan a surprise date.

If he's into gadgets, hobbies, or tools, invest in that.

The best gifts aren't about money, they're about intention.

Privacy & Shared Space

Taking care of a man also means making him feel secure in your space. Men need to know their presence is honored and not diluted by outsiders who don't belong.

Exes should not have unrestrained access to you. If children are involved, that's one thing, but casual conversations, emotional venting, or "just checking in" is not care, it's confusion.

You should be able to hand your phone over to your man or husband with zero notice and not flinch. The only thing he should stumble across is the group chat where you joked about him tripping a little.

Protecting your space is part of caring for him, he should never feel like outsiders are competing for energy, affection, or information that belongs to him.

Creating a Safe Space

Arguments help no one. Raised voices, slammed doors, and defensive words only push intimacy further away. That's why I created what Ryan and I call the Safe Space concept.

When either of us feels triggered, unheard, or needs to bring up an uncomfortable topic, we don't argue in the kitchen, the car, or in front of the kids. We ask for the closet.

Yes, literally, our bedroom closet.

Here's the rule: in the Safe Space, you can't get audibly or visibly upset. You have to sit, listen, and honor the boundaries of that moment.

You cannot interrupt.

You cannot argue or object.

You cannot roll your eyes, sigh, or get defensive.

The only acceptable responses are:

"Okay."

"I didn't know that."

"Thank you for sharing."

That's it. And here's the most important part: it cannot be addressed in the closet. The information can only be processed and discussed later, either before bed that night or within one week.

This rule gives space for emotions to cool, perspective to settle in, and solutions to be found without the chaos of an argument. It's not about ignoring problems, it's about ensuring they're handled with clarity and calm instead of heat and hurt.

Carrying Yourself Well & Honoring His Position

Don't put yourself in situations that jeopardize the whole. Once married, you are two LLCs becoming one corporation, and everything you do represents both of you.

A husband doesn't just take a girlfriend, he takes a wife. And with that title comes responsibility on both sides. Marriage means the union itself becomes the focus. That means:

Your behavior in public reflects on him, just as his reflects on you.

When you go out, remember you represent your man. Carry yourself with class and respect.

Don't flirt, linger, or lock eyes with another man in a way that can be misinterpreted.

In a blended family or any major decision, you don't move solo. If it affects the whole, you consult your husband and come to a reasonable agreement.

Honoring his position means honoring the role you wanted him to be in. You chose him as your leader, your partner, your husband, so his voice carries weight.

Taking care of a man isn't just about rubbing his back or cooking his favorite meal. It's also about respecting the authority of the union you both created.

Crystal Confession

I used to think caring for a man meant exhausting myself to prove I was "good enough." Now I know it's about balance, putting my phone down when he talks, letting him settle before I unload, rubbing his back, giving him a gift that shows I really know him, carrying myself well in public, keeping outsiders from intruding, and respecting the authority of our marriage. That balance is what makes him feel secure and me feel respected.

Crystal Carmen Real Talk

Taking care of a man isn't about perfection, it's about presence. It's being mindful of his energy, generous with affection, intentional with gifts, protective of privacy, and conscious of how your behavior represents him. It's also about honoring his position as your husband, consulting him on what affects the whole, and respecting the corporation you both agreed to build.

And when you wrap all of that with warmth, love, nurturing, food, understanding, and the ability to ignite not just his body but his mind , you can be sure your man is well taken care of. As I like to call it: Fed and Finished.

- Love is in the details small acts of attention matter more than grand gestures.

- Affection is connection, not weakness.

- Sternness is accountability delivered with grace.

- Gifts and celebrations show intention, not just money.

- Protecting privacy and shared space is part of honoring your man.

- Safe Space conversations create clarity instead of chaos.

- Carrying yourself with class and respecting the authority of your marriage protects the union.

- True care balances love, affection, respect, and representation , leaving him both fed and finished.

Journal Prompts

When I think about "taking care of a man," what comes up first for me , nurturing, exhaustion, fear, or balance? Why?

How do I currently show love in the details? What small things can I do more consistently to let him know I see and appreciate him?

Do I create space for him to decompress, or do I unintentionally overwhelm him after work or when he gets home?

What role does affection (non-sexual and sexual) play in my relationship right now? How can I be more intentional with it?

How comfortable am I with giving sternness in love? Do I hold my man accountable with grace, or do I avoid it out of fear of conflict?

When it comes to gifts, do I choose convenience or intention? What would it look like to plan a gift that makes him feel deeply seen?

How am I protecting the privacy of our relationship? Are there any "outsiders" with too much access to my energy, time, or emotional space?

What would creating a true Safe Space look like in my relationship? How could I introduce or reinforce that concept without resistance?

Do I carry myself in public in a way that honors both me and my man? Where might I need to refine how I represent us as a couple?

If I were to fully embrace the idea of "Fed and Finished," what would that look like in my daily life?

THE AFFIRMATION

We don't chase, we attract

Repeat This Every Day Until He Comes

I am not begging for love.

I am not auditioning for someone's attention.

I am not proving my worth to anyone who can't already see it.

I am whole.

I am healed.

I am her.

I move with softness and strength.

I lead with grace, not games.

I attract with my energy, not my effort.

I will not shrink to be chosen.

I will not settle to feel safe.

I will not perform to be praised.

The man for me is aligned, not assigned.

He is led by vision.

He is driven by care.

He doesn't run from responsibility, he owns it.

Until he arrives, I love myself boldly.

I honor my needs fully.

I protect my peace unapologetically.

I am not too much.

I am made for more.

The man who is meant for me will not need convincing.

He will feel me before I speak.

He will see me and know.

And he will meet me in purpose, in partnership, and in power.

I am ready.

I am open.

I am already loved.

THE MAN–IFESTO

CRYSTAL CARMEN'S MANIFESTO

For the woman who is done dimming, done settling, and done being confused about her worth.

I am not here to beg for love, earn affection, or convince anyone to choose me.

I do not audition for roles in other people's lives.

I am the main character, and the writer of the damn script.

I will not be ashamed of my power.

I will not be silenced in my softness.

I will not shrink my standards to make room for men who don't know what to do with a woman like me.

I am not just pretty. I am present.

I am not just strong. I am sovereign.

I am not just nurturing. I am needed.

And I will not apologize for demanding what I give:

Consistency.

Respect.

Intention.

Romance.

Reciprocity.

And peace.

I don't care how much money you make.

If your character is cheap, we're done before we start.

I don't want a perfect man.

I want a healed one.

A willing one.

A man who knows that leadership doesn't mean control, it means care.

I am not "too much."

I'm exactly right for the man who's done playing.

And until he arrives?

I will date with dignity.

I will love with discernment.

I will lead myself in grace, in glow, and in God.

Because I am a woman of value.

And I know that the man who deserves me... won't need convincing.

He will recognize me.

And he will rise to meet me where I already live.

Bonus: The Mini D.R.I.N.K Guide

B onus Feature: The Mini D.R.I.N.K. Guide
     A Sip Before the Pour

(from Girl, You Need a D.R.I.N.K., releasing Feb 2026)

Part 1: Scenarios to Watch Out For

Everyone loves to think they'd spot the red flags. But when feelings get involved, smart women fall into the same traps every day. Here are 5 of the top 20 scenarios I see over and over and how to spot them before they cost you time, tears, or dignity.

Scenario 3: "He's separated, but we still live together."

What it looked like:

He swore they were "basically done" but still shared a lease, a bed, or bills.

Every update sounded like progress, but somehow she was always still in the picture.

He said he just needed "a little more time."

What it likely meant:

You were the side story, not the main event.

He had no plan to fully separate.

He wanted the comfort of a wife at home and the thrill of you on the side.

Crystal's Confession

When I was dating, I made myself a rule: if he's still under the same roof as another woman, I don't care if they're fighting like cats and dogs, he's unavailable. "Separated but living together" is just code for "I want to have my cake and eat it too."

Scenario 7: "I don't want a relationship right now."

What it looked like:

He made it clear upfront, but still wanted your time, your body, your energy.

He called and texted daily, like a boyfriend, but without any titles.

He gave just enough hope to keep you hooked.

What it likely meant:

He wanted all the benefits without responsibility.

He told you his intentions, you just didn't want to believe him.

You became the placeholder until he was ready for someone else.

Crystal's Confession

Ryan and I were dating, he wasn't running around saying, "I'm looking for a wife right this second." What he was was open. Open to love, open to seeing where things could go.

But here's the difference: when he looked at me, he realized I wasn't looking for casual. I gave him that look the one that says, "I'm not here to waste time." And instead of pulling away, he leaned in. He realized, "I could do this again... with her."

Scenario 10: "She's just my friend."

What it looked like:

He spent more time texting her than you.

You only met her in passing, or worse, never at all.

He got defensive every time you asked questions.

What it likely meant:

She wasn't just a friend.

Or even if she was, he wasn't respecting you by making you feel secure.

A high-value man won't let another woman cause confusion in his relationship.

Crystal's Confession

In my past, I let "just friends" slide more than once. And every time, I regretted it. Later, I realized that when a man is serious, there's transparency. When Ryan and I were dating, I knew his friends, and he made sure I felt included , not left guessing.

Scenario 15: "I'm too busy with work."

What it looked like:

He canceled dates last minute because "something came up at the office."

He never planned ahead because "my schedule is crazy right now."

He said he wanted a relationship someday but right now "work had to come first."

What it likely meant:

You weren't a priority.

Work was a shield for emotional distance.

If he really wanted you, he'd make space.

Crystal's Confession

When Ryan and I were dating, he was already a pharmaceutical scientist at a major company. His job was demanding, experiments ran late, deadlines were brutal, and the pressure was constant.

And yet... he still found time to send me a text. He still called me after work. Because when a man values you, "busy" doesn't erase you from his day.

Scenario 19: "We're not exclusive, but I act like we are."

What it looked like:

He wanted you to treat him like a girlfriend, but refused to give you the title.

He got jealous if you talked to other men, but claimed he had every right to date around.

He said, "Why ruin a good thing with labels?"

What it likely meant:

He wanted exclusivity from you without giving it back.

He didn't see you as the one, just as one of many.

Real men looking for commitment won't play the "titles don't matter" game.

Crystal's Confession

I once allowed myself to be in one of these "situationships." He didn't want a title, but he wanted all the benefits of one. I tried to tell myself being the favorite was enough, but it never was.

Here's the lesson: when a man is serious, there's no confusion. He won't hide behind "labels don't matter." Claiming you is part of how he loves you.

Part 2: The Top 3 Places to Meet High-Value Men

Everyone wants to know where the good men are. Baby, they're not hiding they're just not where you've been looking. If you only fish in ponds full of bottom-feeders, don't be shocked when you keep pulling out catfish.

Here are 3 of my top spots for meeting high-intention men the ones who actually have something to offer besides smooth talk and sneakers.

1. The Races (Horse or Car)

Horse races and car races attract men with disposable income, a taste for thrill, and a love for tradition or engineering. Pro Tip: Dress with intention a chic hat and heels at the track, a sleek look at the car races.

2. Happy Hours Near Corporate Buildings

Post-work happy hours around corporate hubs are like rush hour for eligible men. Pro Tip: Sit at the bar, not the booth. Smile. Be open. Men notice the woman who looks approachable.

3. Tailgates & Libraries

Tailgates: Men are relaxed, social, and open to conversation.

Libraries: Men who value discipline, intelligence, and growth. Pro Tip: At a tailgate, bring fun energy. At a library, keep it soft and light.

Part 3: 5 Life-Upgrades That Raise Your Vibe

Your energy introduces you before you ever open your mouth. If you keep dating the same man in a different body, or you keep attracting men who drain you, this part is for you. Your vibe creates your tribe, and if you want high-value love, you have to first be high-value with yourself.

Here are 5 upgrades that have nothing to do with chasing a man and everything to do with upgrading you.

1. Invest in Your Healing

If you find yourself repeating cycles, either hire a coach or a therapist. Healing clears out the junk so you stop mistaking chaos for chemistry.

A healed woman doesn't fall for a man's potential. She evaluates him on his present reality. That's power.

2. Move Your Body (for You, Not Him)

Even light exercise moves your lymphatic system, keeps your skin glowing, balances your hormones, and stabilizes your mood.

When you feel better, you radiate differently. Confidence is magnetic. Men pick up on it, but more importantly, you feel it.

3. Buy Yourself the Damn Flowers

Don't wait for a man to validate your worth with a bouquet. Buy them yourself. Place them where you'll see them every day.

Treat yourself the way you want to be treated so you're already fluent in love when it arrives.

4. Date Yourself at Brunch (Alone)

Going solo in a social setting makes you approachable and grounded. Instead of filling the silence with chatter, you taste your food, sip your drink, and actually notice who's around you.

Learning to enjoy your own company is one of the most magnetic qualities a woman can have.

5. Curate Your Space Like It's Sacred

Your home is either draining you or fueling you. Upgrade it with candles, luxury sheets, nourishing food, and intentional design.

When you walk into a space that feels beautiful, you carry that energy out into the world.

Bonus Tip: Style Isn't Your Problem, But I've Got You

The right man isn't choosing you based on Gucci vs Zara. It's your energy he feels first.

But how you present yourself still matters. If you need help, shop my Looks to Love list on my Amazon Storefront. I handpicked pieces that vibe with feminine, magnetic energy so you can feel good walking into any room.

These are just the first sips. The full 20 scenarios, all 8 places, and all 10 upgrades will be waiting for you in Girl, You Need a D.R.I.N.K., launching January.

Make sure you're on my list at CrystalCarmen.com and in the Bougee Behavior group so you don't miss the preorder.

Pour The First Kiss

Love and Chemistry Cocktail & Mocktail

The inspiration for this recipe comes from Ryan and my very first kiss. I was showing him the theater room, and the energy between us was electric the kind of current you can't fake. Just as I was about to leave the room, he kissed me. Normally, I would've been livid at someone moving in uninvited. But this wasn't just anyone, and this wasn't just any kiss. The way he gently pulled me in, the pause before his lips met mine... it was like a scene straight out of a movie.

That kiss wasn't just a kiss, it was a beginning. The kind that makes you savor the moment forever. And that's what this drink is about: the sweetness, the sparkle, the pause that changes everything.

<u>Cocktail Version</u>

Ingredients

2 oz champagne or prosecco

1 oz vodka (vanilla or plain)

1 oz fresh strawberry purée

½ oz lemon juice (freshly squeezed)

½ oz simple syrup

Strawberry slice or edible flower for garnish

Instructions

Shake vodka, strawberry purée, lemon juice, and simple syrup with ice.

Strain into a chilled coupe glass.

Top with champagne or prosecco.

Garnish with a strawberry slice or an edible flower.

Mocktail Version

Ingredients

2 oz sparkling water or non-alcoholic sparkling wine

1 oz strawberry purée

½ oz lemon juice (freshly squeezed)

½ oz honey syrup (or agave for vegan option)

Strawberry slice for garnish

Instructions

Shake strawberry purée, lemon juice, and honey syrup with ice.

Strain into a chilled coupe glass.

Top with sparkling water.

Garnish with a strawberry slice.

From Us to You

This recipe is our gift to you a reminder that love can be sweet, playful, and intentional. Whether you sip the cocktail or the mocktail, let this drink be your toast to passion, presence, and that one kiss that changes everything.

Ready to Go Deeper?

This book cracked the door open. Now let's walk all the way through.

You don't have to navigate love, healing, or high-value dating alone. If you're ready to break old cycles, clear out relationship confusion, and attract the kind of love that aligns with the woman you are now... I've got you.

1. Join the Bougee Behavior Community

Be surrounded by like-minded women who are done settling and ready to step fully into their soft, intuitive, empowered energy. Inside my private group, you'll get real-time support, exclusive live sessions, and the sisterhood you didn't know you needed.

Join us on Facebook search: BouGee Behavior

2. Book a 1:1 Crystal Clear Session with Me

Got dating drama? Confused about where you stand with him? Wondering if you're sabotaging your own love life, or just tired of feeling like it's all on you?

Girl Talk.. just you and me.

Book a private, transformational session where we get to the root of what's blocking you from purposeful love and emotional peace. No fluff. No pretending. Just real clarity, strategy, and soul-deep honesty.

This is for the woman who wants:

- To stop repeating cycles

- To love herself and let herself be loved

- To experience a relationship that feels like peace, passion, and purpose combined

Book now at: crystalcarmen.com

About the Author

A bout the Author

Crystal Carmen is not your traditional dating coach, she's a former celebrity makeup artist turned relationship strategist, soft life preacher, and feminine energy expert who teaches women how to stop performing for love and start receiving it.

She is also a scientist and researcher, specializing in the physical and psychological effects of trauma on the body and how those impacts shape the way we date, connect, and choose partners. Her work dives deep into the nervous system, feminine-masculine energy dynamics, and the often overlooked biological consequences of emotional wounding and misaligned relationships.

After surviving her own trauma, reclaiming her voice, and building a life that looks as good as it feels, Crystal now helps women stop chasing emotionally unavailable men and start attracting love that honors their softness, ambition, and intuition.

She's the founder of BouGee Behavior, a lifestyle community for women who are done begging, building with boys, and settling for struggle love. Her teachings blend science and soul, mixing feminine communication, trauma-informed strategy, spiritual alignment, and sacred self-worth.

Whether she's hosting live events, guiding women in one-on-one sessions, or serving married girl realness online, her message stays the same:

Be soft, be spoiled, be selective, and don't you dare apologize for it.

Crystal lives in Pennsylvania with her brilliant, handsome husband Ryan, where they build businesses, raise children, and co-create a beautifully balanced life of passion, creation, and purpose.

Ready for Real Love?

Book a **Private 1:1 Session** with Crystal.

Get clarity, strategy, and the kind of no-nonsense truth that helps you stop repeating cycles and finally attract love that resonates.

www.crystalcarmen.com

Want My Advice Without the Pressure?

Submit your situation and receive a **Crystal Clear Video Reply**
Personalized, straight-to-the-point advice you can replay anytime.
www.crystalcarmen.com

Still Too Shy? Spill the Tea Anonymously.

Submit your story **anonymously** for a chance to be featured in my *Spill the Tea* segment. If selected, I'll answer your question publicly (without name or location) so you get the guidance you need while helping other women too.

Email: spillthetea@gmail.com

Join the community: Pretty on Purpose on Facebook

Follow Crystal's journey on Instagram & YouTube: @crystalcarmen

Reader Review Request and Sneak Peek

If this book lifted you or resonated in anyway, please take a moment out of your busy day. to eave a review. Your words help another woman choose love that looks like provision, protection, partnership, and peace. A few sentences is perfect.

Share one insight you used, one change you made, or one chapter you loved.

Thank you for helping this message reach the women who need it most.

When a woman leaves a review, another woman finds her way to provision, protection, partnership, and peace.

What to share

• One insight that changed your energy

• One situation you felt resonated with you

• One chapter or Crystal Confession that stayed with you
• One tip or concept you tried and what happened

Where to leave it

• Apple Books: open the book page and tap Write a Review
• Amazon: open the book page, select Write a customer review

Thank you for helping this message reach the woman who needs it tonight.

Preview of the Next Book.....

Sneak Peek: Girls You Need a D.R.I.N.K.

You've got the clarity now but clarity without action is just another self-help book collecting dust. That's why *Girls You Need a Drink* is your next move.

Inside, I'm spilling the secrets of my **5-Level Rotational Dating Program™** the same strategy that I developed that helped me and had my girlfriends going from first date to fiancé in six months flat.

I won't give it all away here (you'll have to grab the book for that), but just know this: once you start playing by *my* conditions, men will be falling in love faster than you can swipe left... and the one will make it clear he's not letting you go.

This isn't about juggling men for fun. It's not about being promiscuous, it's about using feminine power, boundaries, and energy to make sure you never waste another year on the wrong guy.

So, finish your drink, fix your lipstick, and get ready.
Because *Girls You Need a D.R.I.N.K* isn't just about dating, it's about dating with strategy, dating with joy, and dating for the ring.

WORK WITH CRYSTAL

You do not have to guess alone. If you want my eyes and my energy on your exact situation, choose the option that fits you best.

Private one on one session

Bring your dating or marriage situation. We will identify patterns, set standards, and map your next three moves so you feel clear and calm. Book at: crystalcarmen.com

Crystal Clear video answer

Not ready for a full session. Send your situation and I will record a personalized direct video reply with your next steps and if neccesary what to say or text scripts to use. Perfect when you want fast clarity on situation.

Spill the Tea anonymously

Too shy to be seen. Submit your situation without your name. If selected, I will post the answer for the community so you learn and other women learn with you.

Soft Life Scanner

A dating energy audit that reviews your profiles, updates your photos, bio, vibe, and boundaries so you attract a provider type man who values partnership and peace.

Scan the QR codes or visit crystalcarmen.com to choose your path.

Scan Me

LAST MINUTE THOUGHTS

T HE FINAL WORD
So close this book, baby.
Not because it's over, but because it's only the beginning
The standard has been set.
The soft era is here.
And the love you desire?
Is already on its way.
from Crystal, with love.

Elegance walks in before you. It is not a costume or a performance. It is presence. It is the quiet decision to move with grace and to pair that grace with real boundaries. It is choosing a life where your femininity is honored, your standards are clear, and the way you love is intentional.

All throughout these pages, I told the truth the way I live it. I shared my own confessions, client stories, and the lessons I keep learning in my current marriage. Ryan and I do love in real time. We are not perfect. We don't pretend to be. We are purposeful. That is the difference. Purpose is what turns softness into strength and turns romance into partnership.

If you take anything from this book, let it be this. Elegance is a daily practice. It is how you place your phone down and lift your eyes. It is how you let a man open the door, how you stand at the side of your chair and receive the gesture, how you allow the coat to be placed, the drop at the entrance, the order placed for you after you share what you want. It is how you walk the stairs. It is how you speak and how you listen. These are not small things. They are signals. They tell the world how to treat you and they tell your man how to show up.

Choose softness with a spine. Choose standards with warmth. Choose a love that looks like provision, protection, partnership, and peace. When you carry yourself with value, the right man rises. When you lead yourself with wisdom, your life rises.

I wrote this for the woman who is ready to be unforgettable without being loud. For the wife who wants to deepen what she already has. For the woman who has not met him yet but is done shrinking. I am cheering for you. Ryan is cheering for you. And when you walk into your next room with your shoulders back and your spirit calm, the room will cheer for you too.

Now go be the presence you were meant to be.

SHUT UP AND LOOK PRETTY

With love,
Crystal Carmen Caple